wire & glass

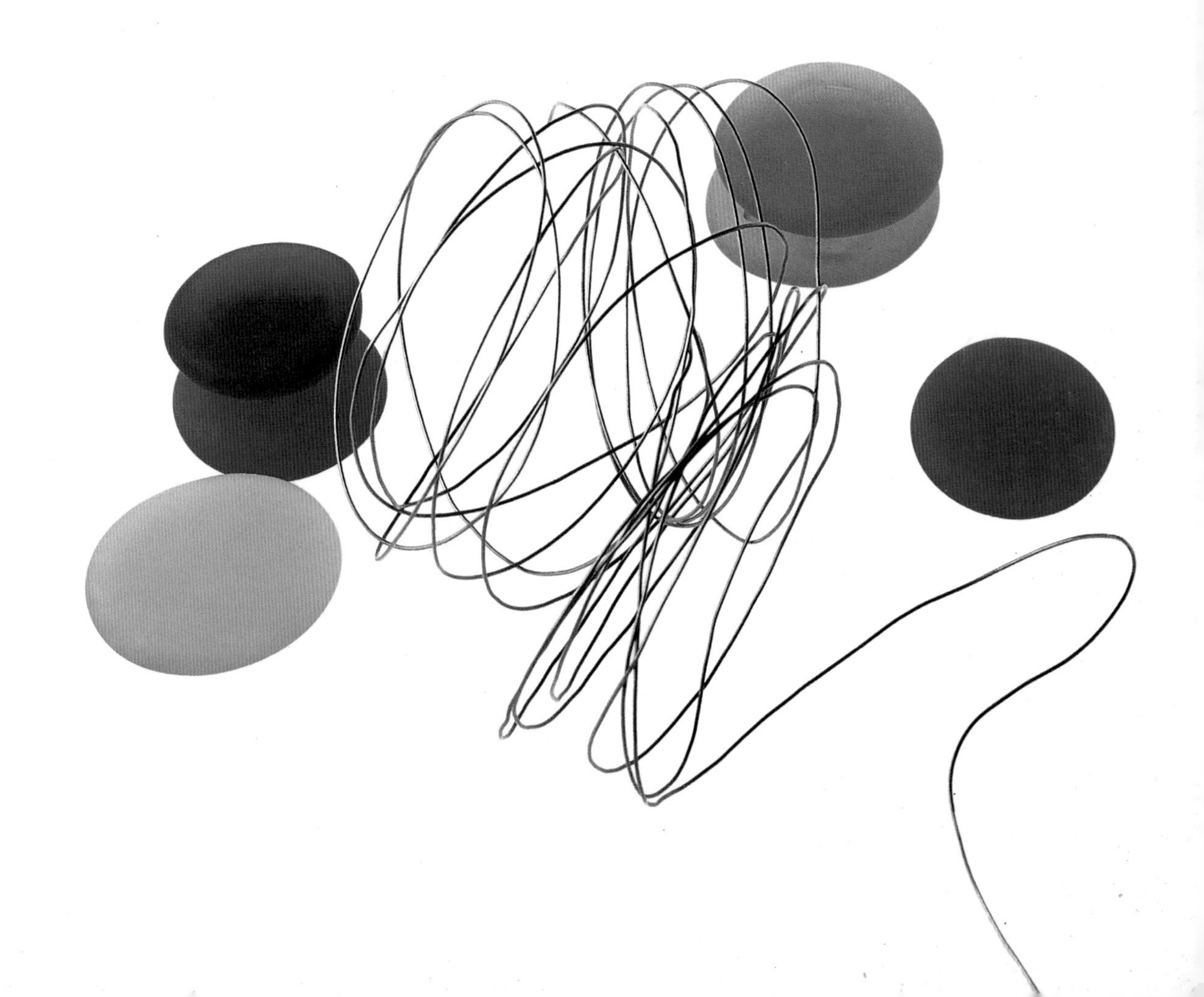

First published in North America in 2001 by
North Light Books
an imprint of F&W Publications, Inc.
1507 Dana Avenue
Cincinnati, OH 45207
1-800/289-0963

Library of Congress Cataloguing-in-Publication Data Is Available.

ISBN: 1-58180-199-8

Project Editor: Jane Ellis
Editor: Michelle Pickering
Designer: Georgina Rhodes
Photographer: Peter Williams
Indexer: Judy Batchelor

Colour reproduction by Global Colour, Malaysia
Printed by Dai Nippon Printing Company

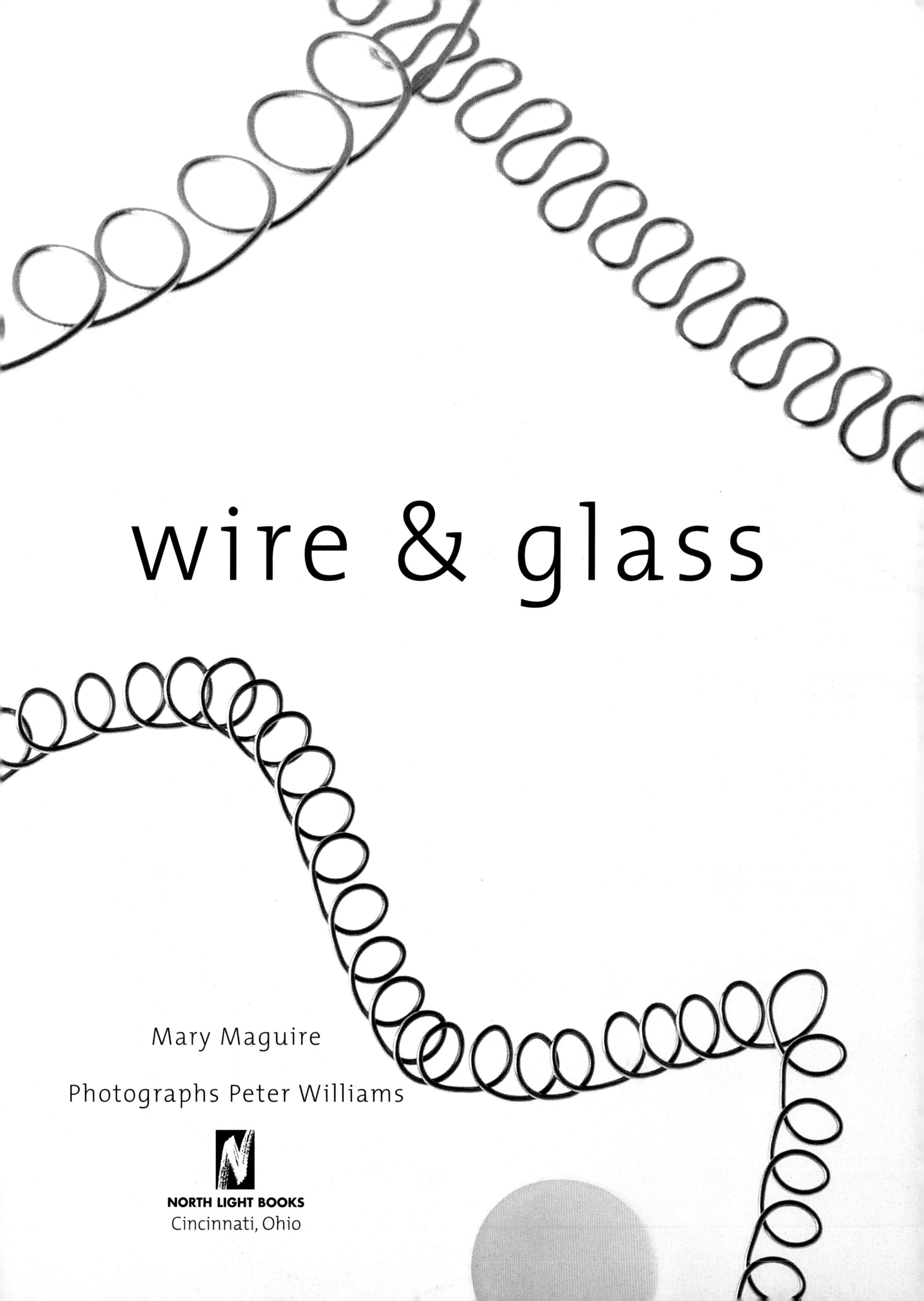

wire & glass

Mary Maguire

Photographs Peter Williams

NORTH LIGHT BOOKS
Cincinnati, Ohio

CONTENTS

INTRODUCTION

The ancient but long-neglected craft of wirework has recently re-emerged with many new applications, fresher and brighter than ever before. It has become an extremely fashionable choice for both functional and decorative objects around the home. In this book we combine the hard linear qualities of wire with the translucent beauty of glass to create a surprizing and delightfully inspiring range of projects – giving the craft of wirework a more contemporary edge. The 22 projects are designed to suit a range of abilities: for the beginner, the butterflies, wall hooks and napkin rings are a good starting place. The more experienced maker may enjoy the challenging lampshade or glass carrier projects. The Basic Techniques section (page 12) shows you how to manipulate wire for both structural and decorative purposes. By bending, joining, binding and coiling, you can add both strength and beauty to a design.

The projects incorporate a range of ready made glass objects, such as marbles and beads, etc., all smoothed edged and user friendly. A list of useful tools is provided on page 8, but for most projects a pair of wire cutters, ordinary and round-nose pliers will suffice. Use this book not only as a pattern book to copy from, but as an inspiration. When you have started bending wire you will see its possibilities: it is an inexpensive, easily available material, so feel free to experiment. There are all sorts of items to make for your home: soap dishes, toothbrush holders, plate racks, baskets, string dispensers, fruit bowls and picture frames. For the garden, bird feeders, topiary framers and plant supports. Once you have got the knack you can go ahead and create your own wonderful wire works.

TOOLS

Here is a selection of useful tools for making wire objects. Although several different types of pliers are specified in the project text because they are the easiest to use for the task in hand, in many cases a pair of ordinary household pliers with cutting edges will be sufficient.

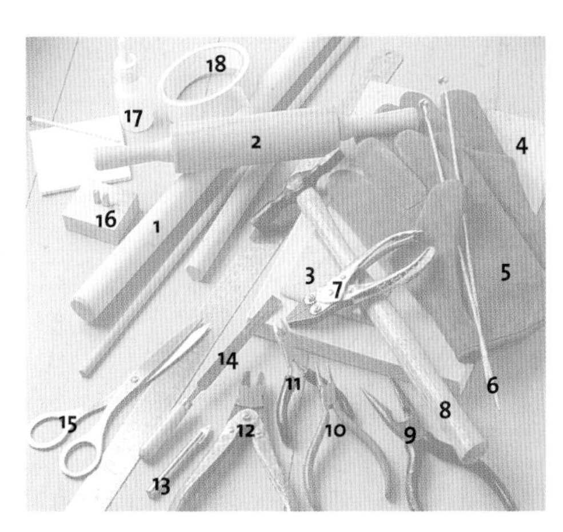

KEY

1 Assorted dowel rods
2 Rolling pin
3 Metal plate
4 Wooden block
5 Protective gloves
6 Knitting needles
7 Parallel pliers
8 Hammer
9 Chain-nose pliers
10 Round-nose pliers
11 Miricle pliers
12 Wire cutters
13 Glass drill bit
14 Metal file
15 Scissors
16 A simple gig
17 Strong glue
18 Masking tape

MATERIALS

Wire is available in many colors and thicknesses. Some are fine and soft enough to knit with like the enameled copper wire shown here. Others, such as galvanized wire, are hard and have to be bent with pliers. The glass used in the projects ranges from sea-worn fragments to Christmas tree baubles.

KEY

1 Enameled copper wire
2 Frosted glass droplets
3 Sea-worn glass shapes
4 Mirror
5 Assorted beads
6 Glass stars
7 Glass disk beads
8 Marbles
9 Chicken wire
10 Christmas tree baubles
11 Recycled glass beads
12 Galvanized wire
13 Florist's wire

BASIC TECHNIQUES

1

WORKING WITH WIRE

Caution must be taken when working with wire. Use gloves to prevent scratches from sharp ends, and wear a pair of goggles to protect your eyes in case pieces of wire fly into the air when it is cut.

2

DRILLING GLASS

Wear goggles to protect your eyes. Stick a piece of masking tape over the area to be drilled to keep the drill from slipping and hold it securely. If appropriate, clamp the glass with protective cushioning. When drilling a difficult object like this saucer, use removable adhesive mounting pads (Blu-Tack) to hold it in place while drilling. Follow the instructions on the drill bit packaging.

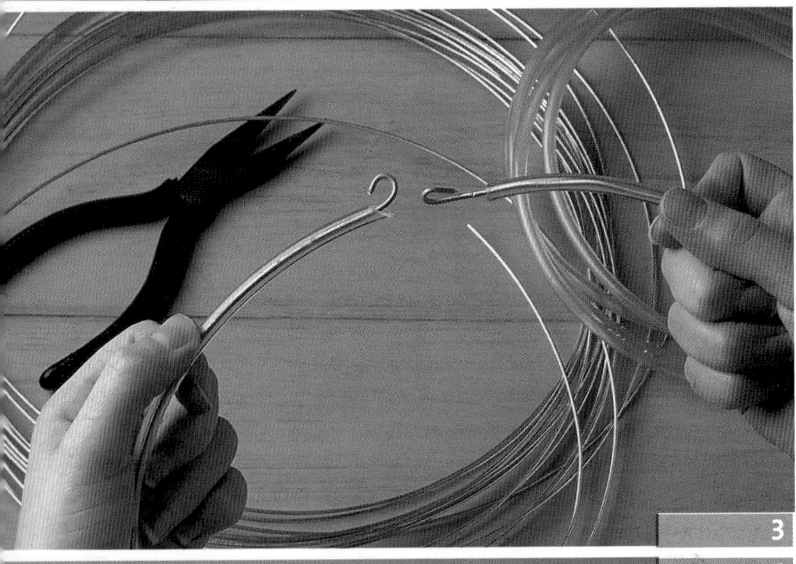

JOINING WIRES

The simplest way to join wires is to use a pair of chain-nose (snipe-nose) or round-nose pliers to form a small loop at the each end of the wire. Link the loops together and squeeze them closed with the pliers.

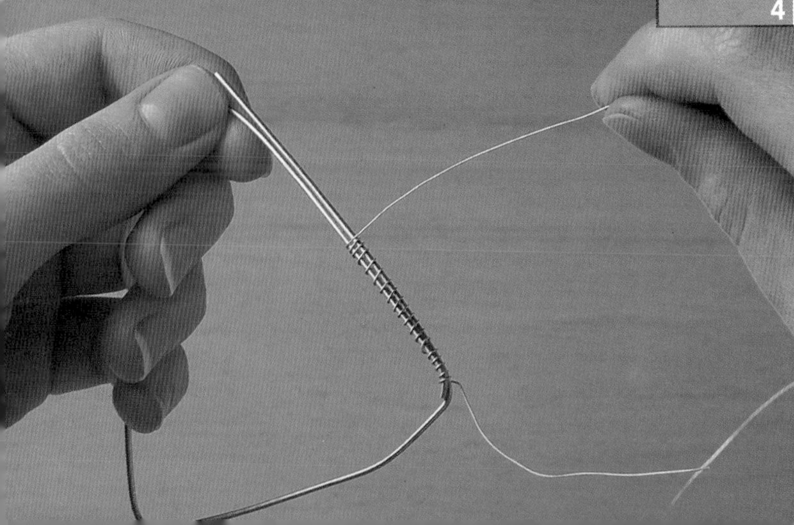

4

BINDING WIRES

Another way to join wires is to bind them together. Place the wires side-by-side, then bind them together by wrapping a length of finer wire tightly around them.

5

TWISTING WIRE

Take a length of wire and loop it around a door handle. Wrap the loose ends securely around a piece of dowel, a coat hanger, or something similar. Keeping the wire taut, turn the dowel around until you achieve the required tension in the wire. Do not overwind or the wire may snap. Take care when releasing the wire because the excess tension will cause it to spin.

6

FORMING SCROLLS

Use round-nose pliers to form a small circle at both ends of a piece of wire. Holding one of the circles with the pliers, wind the length of wire around to form an evenly spaced spiral. Do the same at the other end, working in the opposite direction.

7

FORMING DOUBLE-ENDED SPIRALS

Make double-ended spirals in the same way as scrolls, but bend both ends of the wire in the same direction so that the spirals face each other. If you need to produce spirals of a precise size and shape, draw a template that you can check the wire against.

8

FORMING HEARTS

Make a double-ended spiral with sufficient straight wire between the two spirals to form the body of the heart. Place a finger in the center of the straight length of wire and push the coiled ends together with your thumbs. For a more pointed tip, bend the wire around round-nose pliers instead of your fingers.

5

6

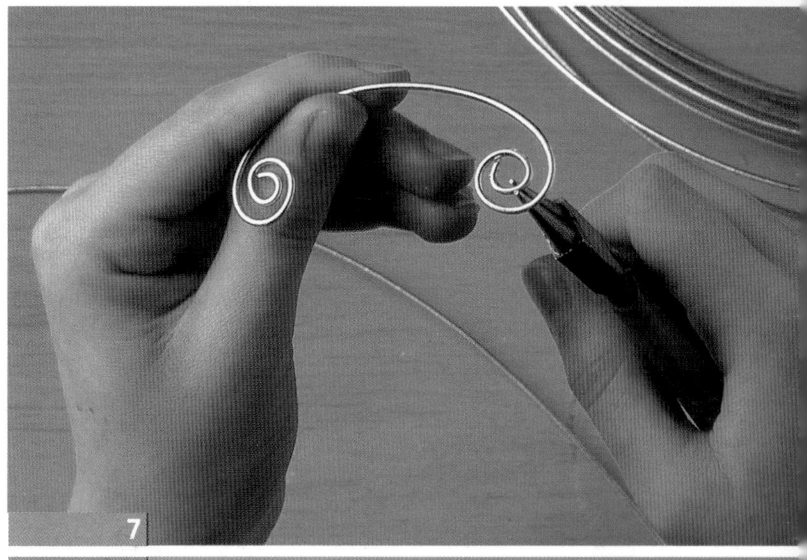
7

8

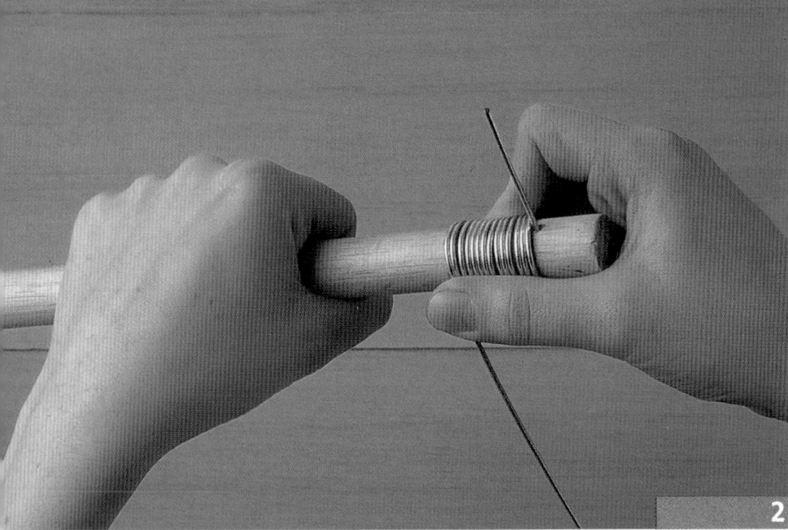

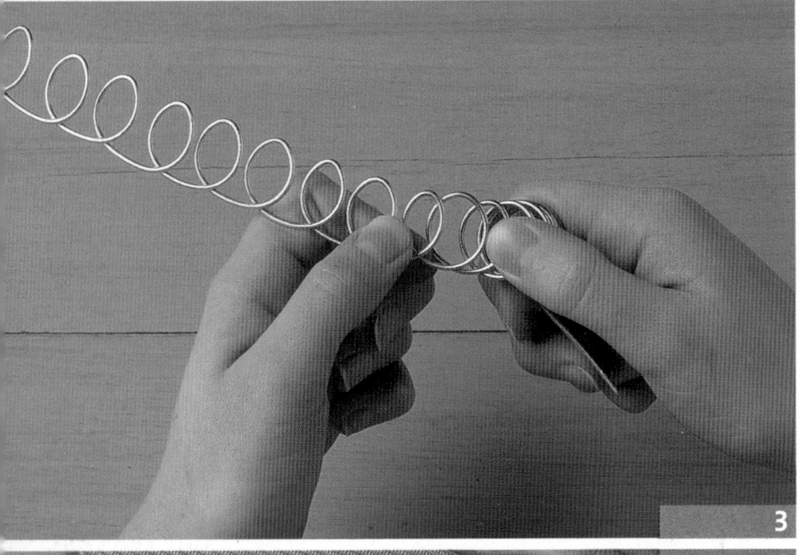

1

MAKING A FLATTENED COIL

Drill a hole through the end of a piece of dowel, then rub a piece of candle over the dowel so that the wire will slide off it more easily after coiling. Thread the end of the wire through the hole in the dowel to keep it in place while coiling.

2

Using your thumb to brace the wire against the dowel, twist the dowel around until you achieve a tight, even coil of wire. Gradually slide your thumb along the dowel as the coil lengthens. To remove the finished coil, cut off the end of the wire that is threaded through the hole in the dowel and twist the coil off.

3

Extend the coil out sidewise by gripping it firmly between both thumbs and pulling it out to the side so that the loops lie side by side.

4

Place the extended coil of wire on a cloth (to protect your work surface) and flatten it with a rolling pin, as the wire may emboss its pattern onto the wood.

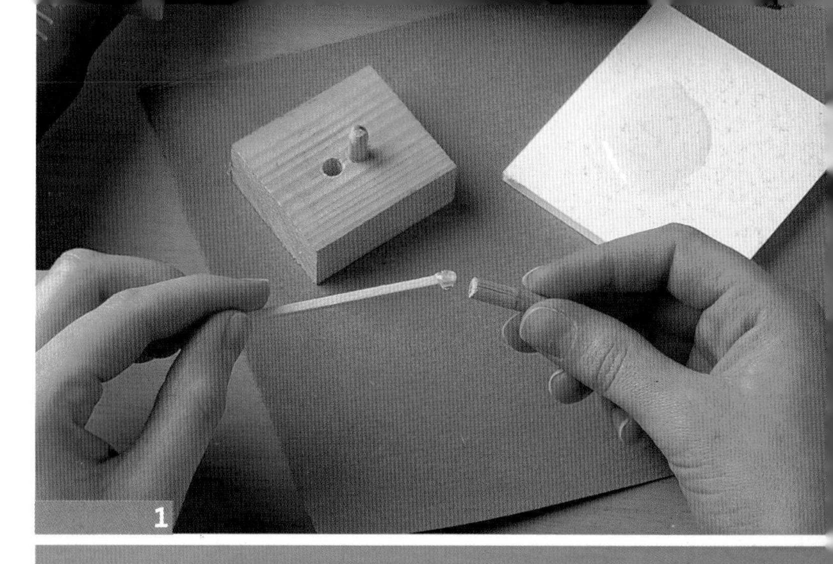
1

1

MAKING WIGGLY WIRE

Decide the depth of curves you require, then mark two points on a piece of wood this distance apart. Make two small pegs from dowel and drill two holes in the piece of wood at the marked points large enough to accommodate the pegs. Glue the pegs in position.

2

2

The finished wooden structure is called a gig. For small loops, use pegs made from thin dowel; for larger loops, use thicker dowel. Try using different thicknesses of wire for different effects.

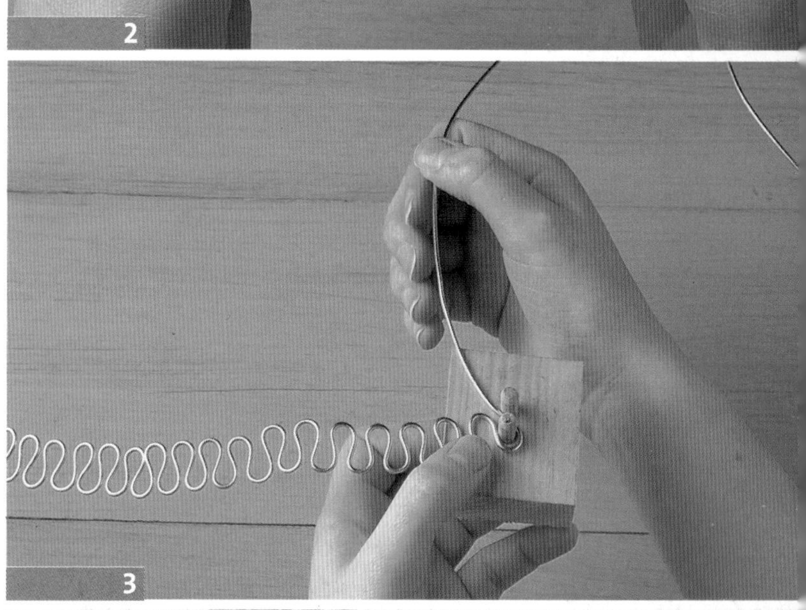
3

3

Hold the gig firmly in one hand, with the two pegs running in a perpendicular line to your body. Using your thumb to hold the end of the wire firmly against the block of wood, bring the remaining length of wire down toward the bottom peg at a right angle and bend it around the base of the peg. Then bend the wire up between the two pegs and around the top peg. Lift the curled wire off the pegs and move it to the side so that you can repeat the process to create two more curls. Continue until you have achieved the required length of wiggly wire.

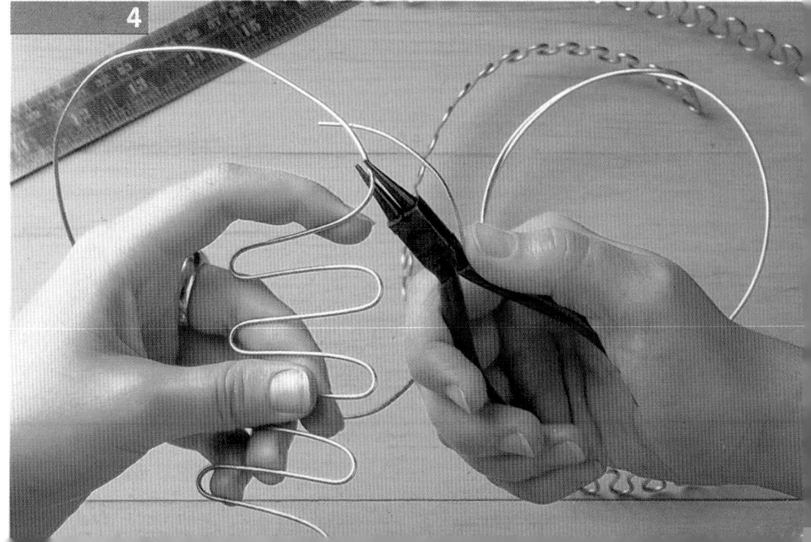
4

4

Instead of using a gig to make wiggly wire, you can do it freehand, using round-nose pliers to bend the wire. To make sure that the depth of the curls is consistent throughout, mark the required depth at regular intervals along the straight wire before bending it. Use your fingers to gauge the width of the loops.

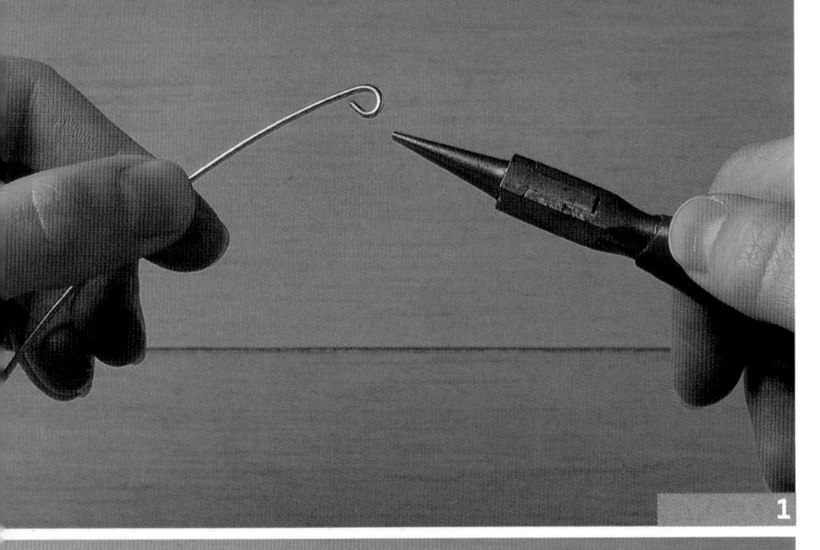

1

MAKING SPIRALS

Hold the end of the wire with a pair of round-nose pliers and twist the length of the wire around the tip of the pliers to form a small loop.

2

For an open spiral, hold the central loop with the pliers and continue to twist the wire into a spiral. Brace the length of the wire between your thumb and forefinger to control it and keep the spiral smooth and even.

3

For a closed spiral, hold the central loop flat between a pair of parallel pliers (ordinary household pliers will do if you do not have a pair of parallel pliers). Wind the wire into a spiral, repositioning the wire between the jaws of the pliers as necessary to keep it flat.

MAKING A COILED SPIRAL

Drill a hole through the end of a piece of dowel, rub the dowel with some candle wax, and thread the end of the wire through the hole (see page 14, step 1). Twist the wire around the dowel to form a tight coil, then remove it from the dowel (see page 14, step 2).

2

Holding the coil firmly in one hand, use the thumb and index finger of your other hand to bend each loop off the tight coil of wire. Keep the space between each loop even by gauging it with your fingertip.

3

As you bend off each loop of the coil, the wire will naturally work itself into a spiral. Continue until you have finished the whole coil.

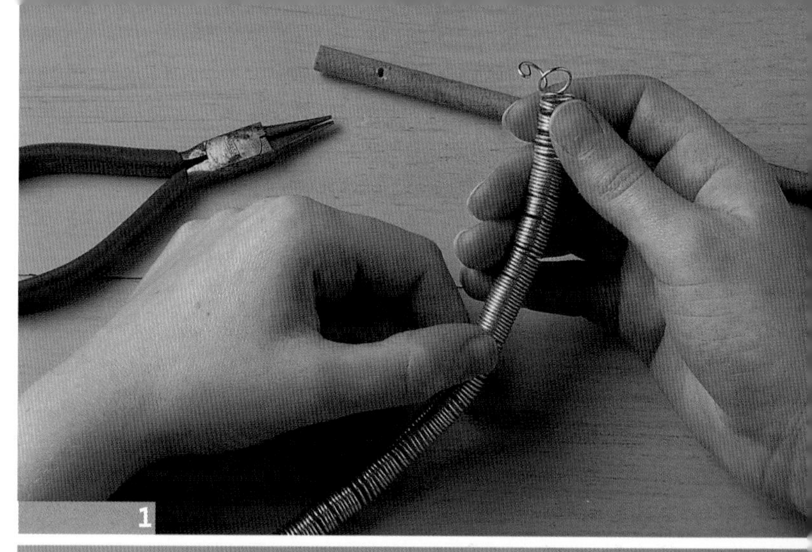

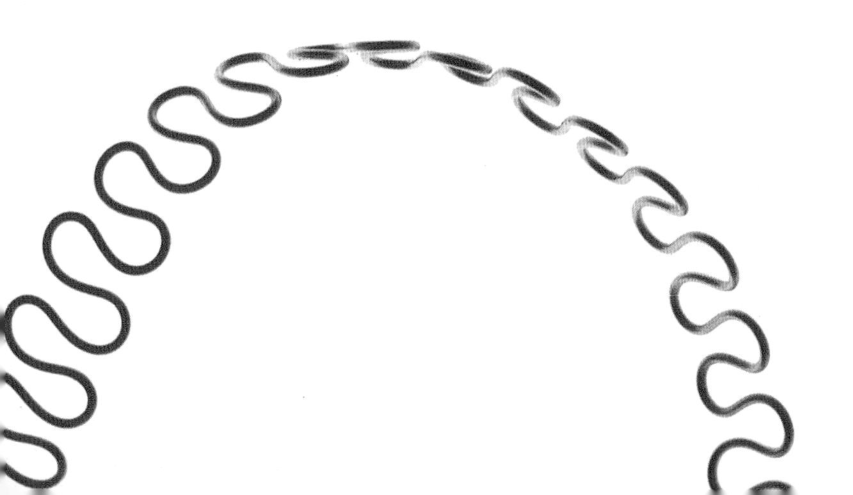

BEADED BUTTERFLIES

These beautiful beaded butterflies are made from enameled copper wire, which is soft enough to manipulate by hand and therefore ideal for beginners. They can be worn as brooches or hair slides with the appropriate jewelry attachment fixed to the back, or you could make them into decorative houseplant supports by attaching them to canes. They also make ideal gift-wrapping decoration for special presents.

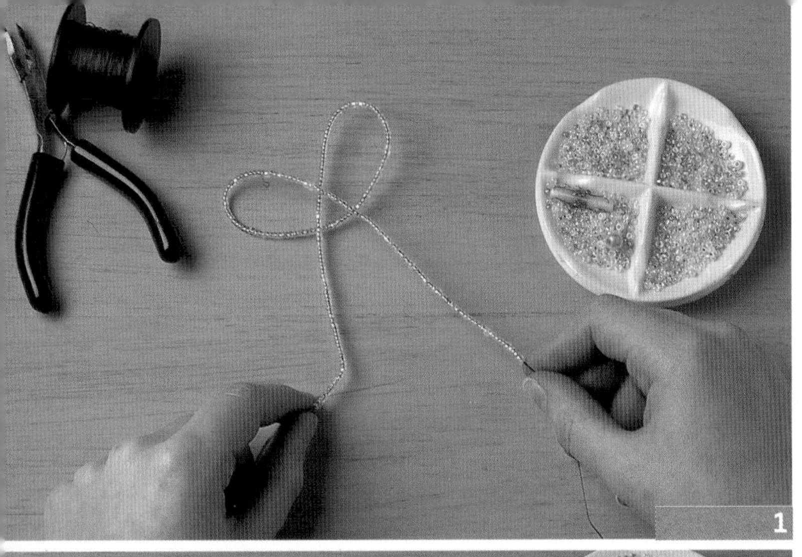

MATERIALS

(for each butterfly)

2ft (60cm) enameled copper wire

Assortment of seed beads

Long bead for the body

Round bead for the head

Strong glue

TOOLS

Household pliers

Cut a 2ft (60cm) length of wire with pliers. Thread seed beads onto the wire until approximately 16in (40cm) is covered with beads. Push the beads into the central section of the wire, then shape the wire into two loops to form the outline of the top section of the wings, as shown.

2

Loop the wire around again to form inner wings, then wrap each end of the wire tightly around the base of the wings to hold them in position. Form two more loops for the lower wings, then wrap the wires around the center point to secure.

3

Twist the remaining lengths of unbeaded wire together to form the body of the butterfly. Slide the long bead for the body and then the round bead for the head onto this twisted length of wire.

4

Bend the body section upward so that it lies flat on top of the wings. Wrap the ends of the wire around the wings on either side to secure the body in place.

5

Spread out the two ends of wire to form antennae and thread a seed bead onto the very end of each one. Secure the beads in place with strong glue.

6

Coil the end wires around these beads to finish off the antennae.

3

4

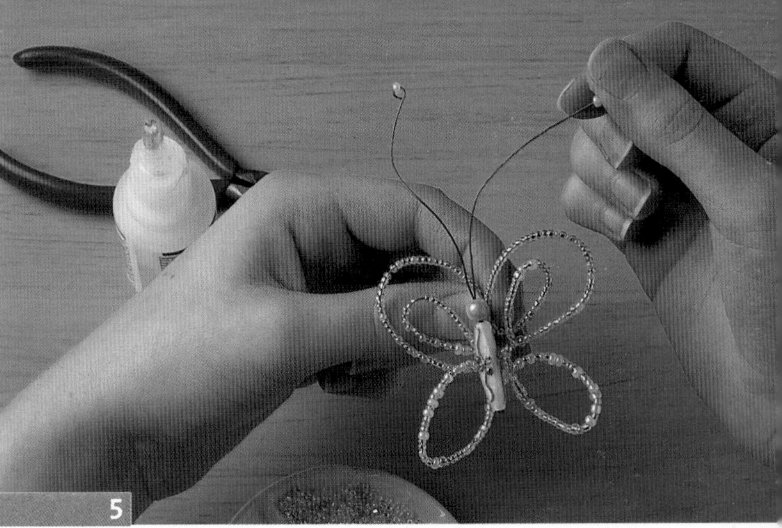

5

6

NAPKIN RINGS

These elegant napkin rings are made simply by threading beads onto wire and coiling it – nothing could be easier. Choose the beads to complement your tableware, or make the napkin rings as a gift for someone else, perhaps a Christmas or wedding present. The beads do not have to be all of the same color, but it is best to use the same type of bead throughout and the same tonal range.

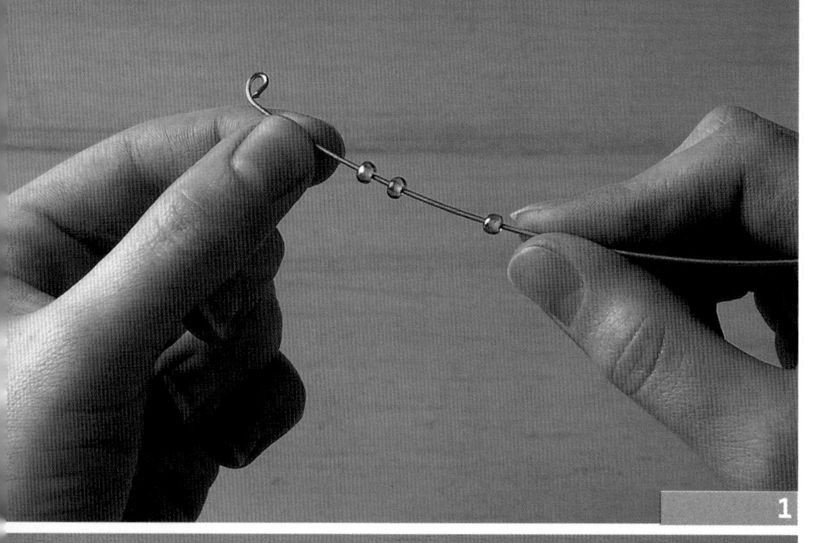

MATERIALS

(for each ring)
0.8mm galvanized wire
Assortment of small beads
2 larger end beads
Strong glue

TOOLS

Wire cutters
Round-nose pliers
Thick dowel

1

Cut a 24in (60cm) length of wire. Holding one end of the wire with pliers, twist the wire around to form a small loop. This will keep the beads from falling off. Start threading the beads onto the wire.

2

Continue to thread beads onto the wire, making sure there are no kinks in the wire to keep the beads from sliding on easily. Leave around 6in (15cm) of wire unbeaded at the end to allow for movement of the beads when the wire is being molded in the next step.

Mold the beaded wire into shape by wrapping the middle section three times around a thick piece of dowel. Gently ease the coil of beaded wire off the dowel.

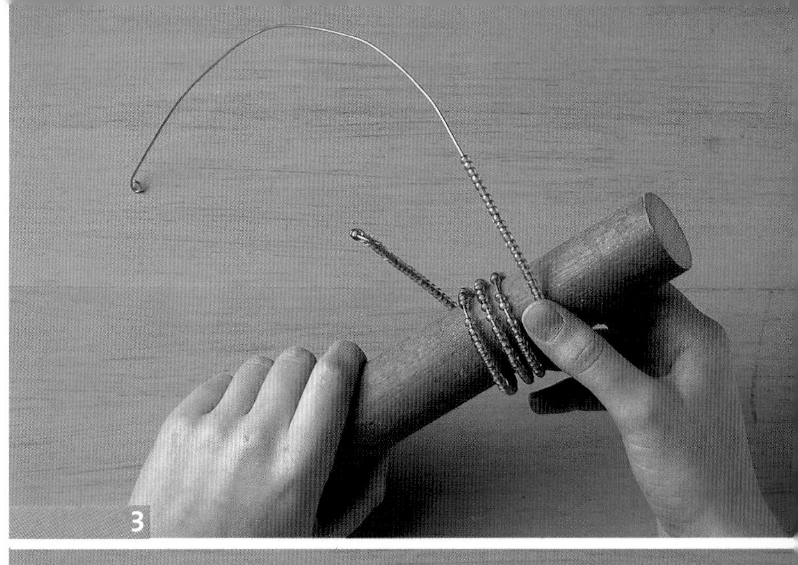

Cut off most of the excess unbeaded wire, then use pliers to form a small loop at the end. Holding the loop firmly with the pliers, form the end of the beaded wire into a scroll. Repeat at the other end of the wire.

5

Snip off the end loops and straighten sufficient wire at each end of the napkin ring to hold the end beads.

6

Fix the end beads in position using strong glue.

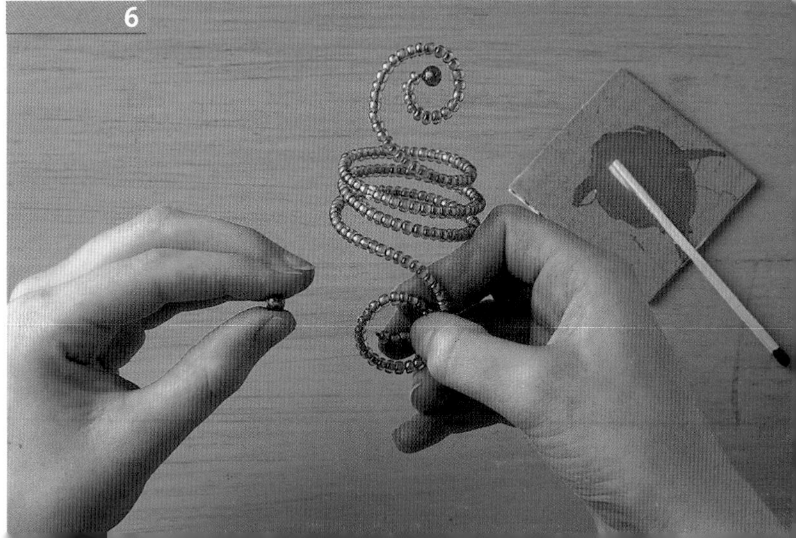

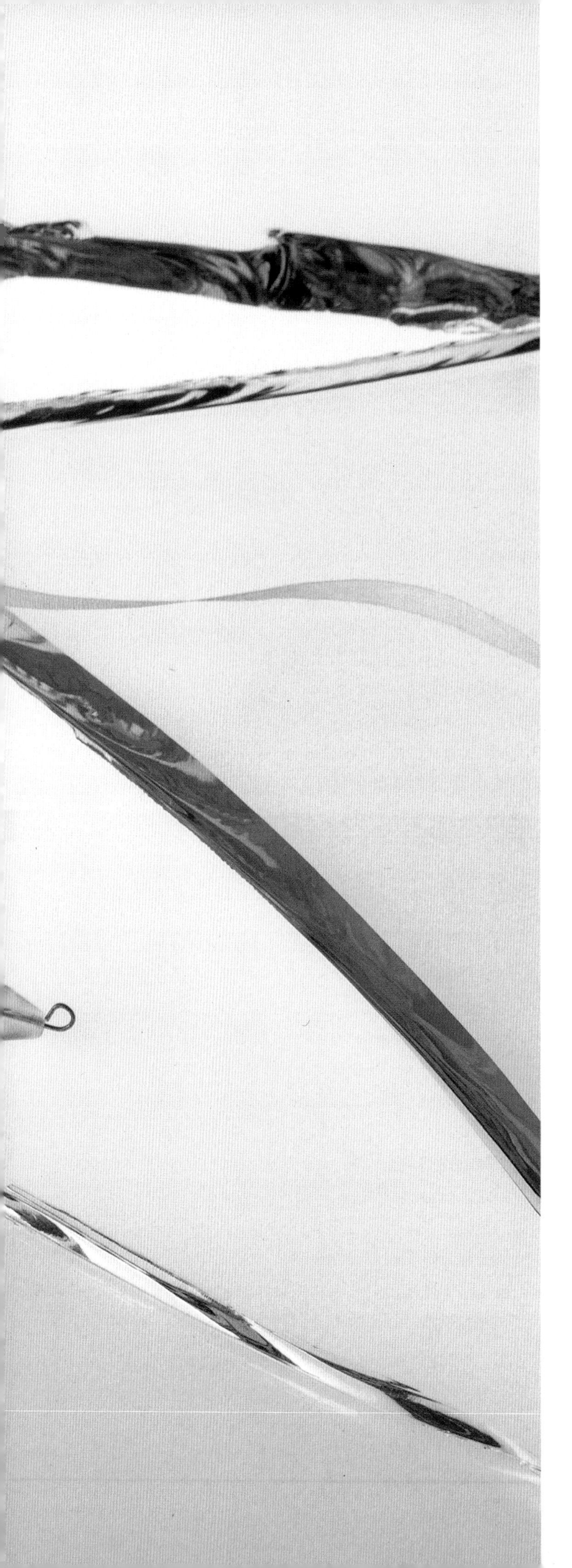

CHRISTMAS STAR

Making Christmas decorations can be very satisfying, whether they are for yourself or a gift. Make sure that the central bead you choose has a hole large enough to accommodate the necessary wires. You can make the star simpler by using fewer wires, or more complex by adding even more wires. A collection of different colored stars looks wonderful hanging on a tree, or catching the light at a window.

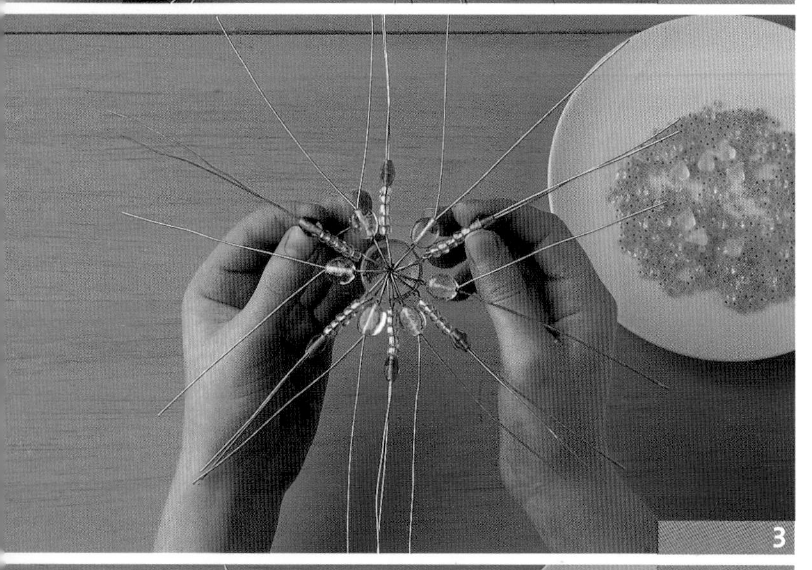

MATERIALS

0.8mm galvanized wire
Central bead with hole big enough to take all the wires
Assortment of small beads and seed beads
12 large beads (half in one color and design, half in another)
6 cone-shaped beads
Crystal droplet

TOOLS

Wire cutters
Round-nose pliers

1

Cut twelve 12in (30cm) lengths of wire. Thread one of the wires through the central bead, bending the wire in half so that the bead is in the middle of the wire. Twist the two ends of the wire together close to the bead to secure it in position. Repeat with the remaining lengths of wire. Spread the wires evenly around the bead.

2

Thread a selection of small beads onto the two ends of every alternate wire, then add a large bead (use the same type of bead for all six wires). If necessary, spread out the two ends of the wires slightly to keep the beads from falling off.

3

Thread the two ends of the remaining empty wires through the remaining large beads, then splay out the two ends to form a V shape.

4

Thread seed beads onto each arm of the six V shapes. Once beaded, use pliers to form a small loop at the end of each wire and bend to a 45-degree angle.

5

Arrange the arms of each V shape so that they meet the adjacent arm of the next V shape to form the points of the star. Fill the remaining doubled wires with seed beads to fit inside the points of the star. If the doubled wire is too thick to go through the beads, cut off one of the wires, wrapping the end tightly around the remaining wire to secure it. When you have finished adding beads, thread the ends of these wires through the overlapping loops of the V shapes, as shown.

5

6

Thread a cone-shaped bead onto the wire projecting through each point of the star and fix in place by forming a loop at the end of each wire using pliers. Hang a crystal droplet from the loop at base point of the star, and attach a ribbon or something similar to the top point for suspending the star.

6

WHIMSICAL FAIRY

This pretty fairy will bring a touch of magic to any occasion. At Christmas she can grace your tree, or suspend her above a birthday cake to preside over the celebrations. Or why not hang her in front of a window where she will be brought to life by passing sunbeams. Her body is made from a wire frame, which holds her delicate glass head in place. Her dress is knitted wire, her glass slippers are beads, and her wings are made from a plastic bottle.

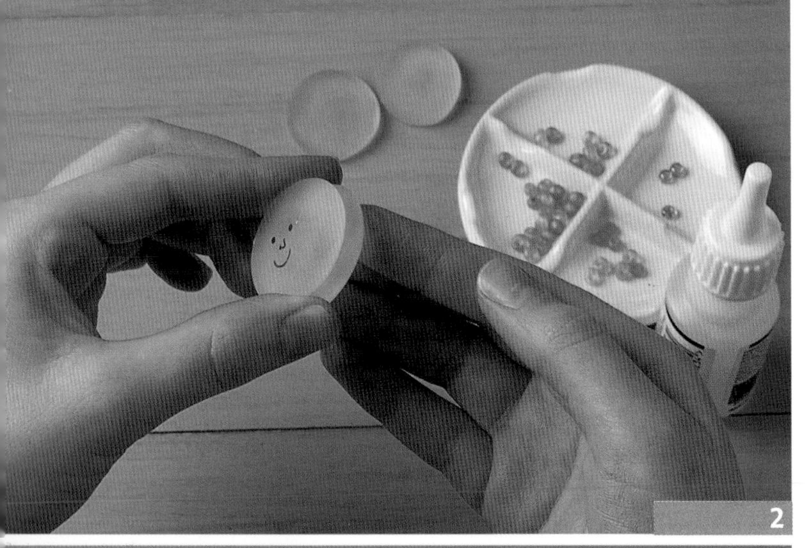

MATERIALS

Seed beads – silver, green and beads for shoes/heart/eyes
Enameled copper wire in pink and silver
Fabric and thin metal foil for dress
2 frosted glass droplets for head
0.7mm, 1.1mm, and 1.5mm galvanized wire
Needle and silver thread
Plastic bottle and glass star

TOOLS

3mm and 4mm knitting needles, scissors

1

For the dress, thread 220 seed beads onto the pink wire and 1,964 beads onto the silver wire (add a few extra beads to allow for errors). Cast on 44 stitches using 3mm needles and pink wire. Knit one row with no beads, then knit four more rows, adding a bead in each stitch on each even-numbered row; knit another ten rows using silver wire, again adding a bead in each stitch on each even-numbered row. Change to 4mm needles and follow the instructions for the evening purse on pages 80–81, starting at the point where 4mm are first used in the purse pattern and using silver wire throughout. Push the finished triangle into shape with your fingers. Cut a triangle of backing fabric and foil the same size as the knitted triangle.

2

To make the face, stick two frosted glass droplets together with strong glue. The groove between the pieces will hold the body in place later. Draw the face using a metallic pen.

3

Wrap lengths of pink wire around a knitting needle to make a long coil. Cut the coil into 1in (2.5cm) lengths. Thread a bead onto one end of each wire coil at a 45-degree angle and bend the end of the wire to secure it in place. Thread the unbeaded ends of each coil onto a length of 1.1mm wire, as shown.

4

Group the coils into a cluster and position them on the center of the wire. Wrap this around the glass head; the wire will fit neatly into the groove between the droplets. Twist the wire together once at the neck position to secure. Spread the wire ends into a V shape, allowing sufficient length for the dress and legs. Thread a shoe bead onto each wire, bending the beads to a 45-degree angle. Wrap the remaining wire tightly around each leg.

5

Cut a length of 1.5mm wire and form a double-ended spiral (see Basic Techniques, page 13). This will become the arms and hands. Attach it near the top of the body by wrapping 0.7mm wire tightly around the arms from wrist to wrist, incorporating the body as shown.

6

Cover the body with the triangle of foil, then sandwich it between the knitted dress and the backing fabric. Stitch these together around the edge with silver thread.

7

Wrap a piece of 0.7mm wire around a glass star and thread seed beads onto the remaining length of the wire to make the handle of a magic wand. For the fairy wings, fold a piece of paper in half and draw one wing from the fold. Cut out and unfold the paper to produce two wings. Draw around the pattern on a plastic bottle and cut out. Make four holes in the center of the wings. Spray paint the wings a different color or give them a frosted edge with glitter paint.

8

Attach the wings to the fairy's back by stitching a big cross-stitch through the holes with thin wire or thread. Attach the wand to the fairy's hand by binding the end of the wire wand around the hand. Suspend a heart bead from the other hand with thread. Gently stretch out the hair coils.

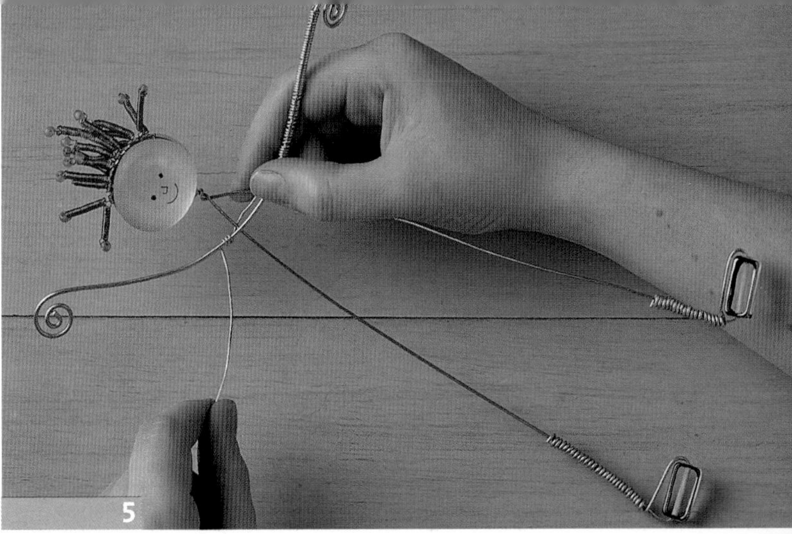

5

6

7

8

Maria

NAME PLAQUE

All you need to make your own name plaque is wire and jewelry pliers. Start by deciding which type of lettering you prefer (bearing in mind that all the letters must be made from a continuous piece of wire). Next practice drawing it out on paper (or computer) until you have a design that you are pleased with. Practice manipulating the wire to get a smooth, even result. The plaque can be used for a door or on a box as shown here, or you could make smaller versions to put on a bag, book or gift. Try incorporating motifs such as flowers, musical instruments or symbols. For a more decorative effect make a beaded surround.

MATERIALS

1.5mm galvanized wire

Glass bead

TOOLS AND EQUIPMENT

Jewelry pliers

Snipe-nose pliers

Pencil and paper

1

Write out your name at the appropriate size and start to bend the wire following the line.

2

Bend the wire under where it travels the same line twice so that it appears as only one line.

3

For the more complicated shapes with tighter bends, use the pliers to make the curves.

4

As you go along, make sure that you are following the line as faithfully as you can.

5

End with a strong curve and use a glass bead to make the dot for the i or just as a feature.

6

You can make a simple cloud shape to frame the name to finish it off.

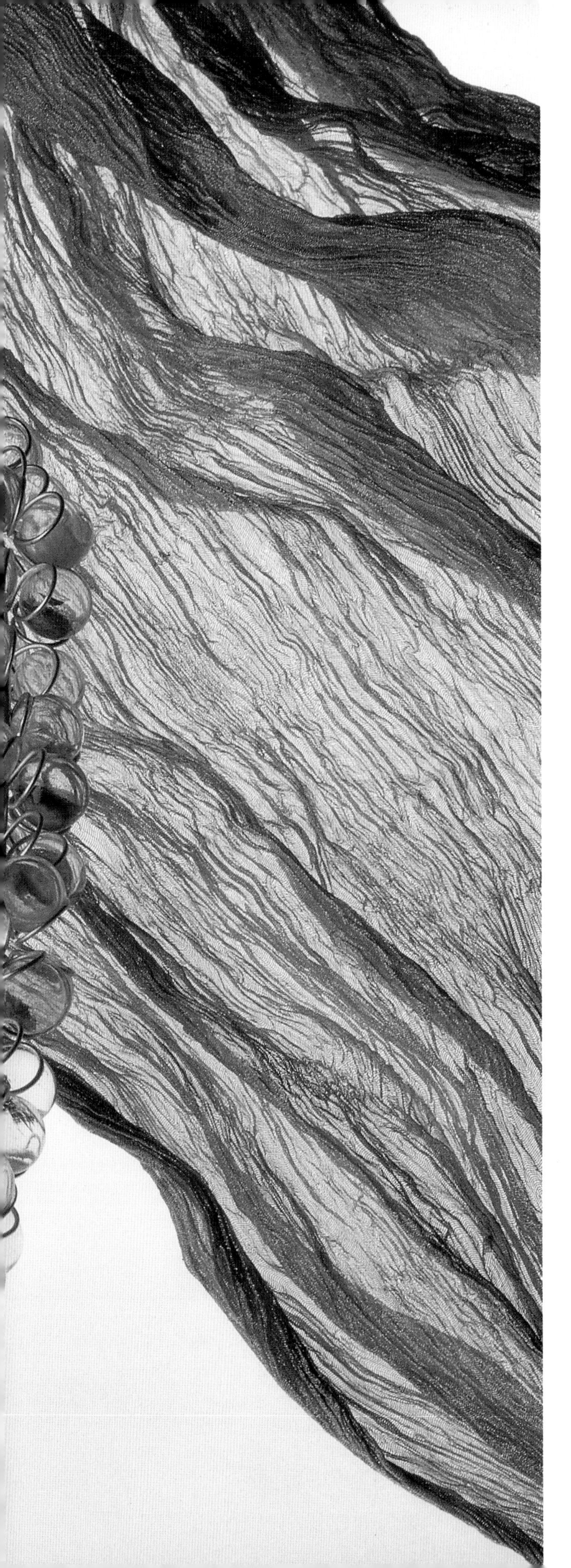

VALENTINE HEART

Simpler to make than it looks, this valentine heart is encrusted with glass marbles suspended between the loops of a coiled wire spiral. It can be hung in front of a window to catch the sun, or placed around a vase of flowers or a cluster of candles to form a stunning centerpiece for a romantic meal for two. For a richer look, try using copper wire combined with red or blue marbles.

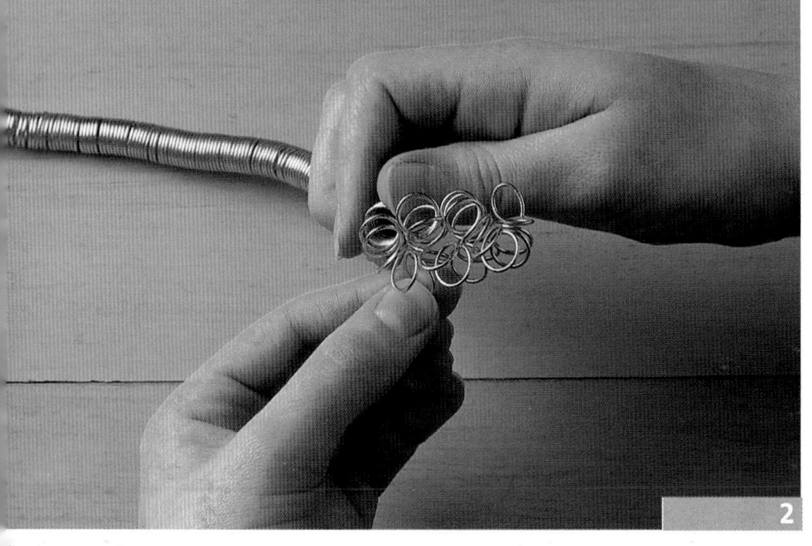

MATERIALS

0.9mm and 1mm galvanized wire
Assortment of small clear marbles
Strong glue

TOOLS

$^{1}/_{2}$in (1cm) dowel
Wire cutters
Round-nose pliers

1

Use 0.9mm wire and the dowel to make a length of wire coil (see Basic Techniques, page 17) suitable for the required heart size. When you have finished, carefully ease the coil off the dowel.

2

Gently open out the tight loops of the wire to form a coiled spiral (see Basic Techniques, page 17).

Insert a length of 1mm wire through the center of the coiled spiral to give it a solid core. Try to keep the wire as central as possible through the middle of the coil for neatness. Allow the wire to project by about 1/2in (1cm) from both ends.

4

Bend the wire coil in half to form a V shape. This will be the bottom point of the heart.

5

Bend the two halves of the coil into curves to form the top of the heart shape. Slip the ends of the core wire through a few spirals on opposite sides of the heart, then use pliers to form the two straight ends into interlocking loops. When the heart is neatly joined, squeeze a few spirals closed to secure.

6

Press marbles between the loops of wire at regular intervals around the heart. They should stay in place if you press firmly, but if they look insecure, glue the underside of each marble at its point of contact with the wire.

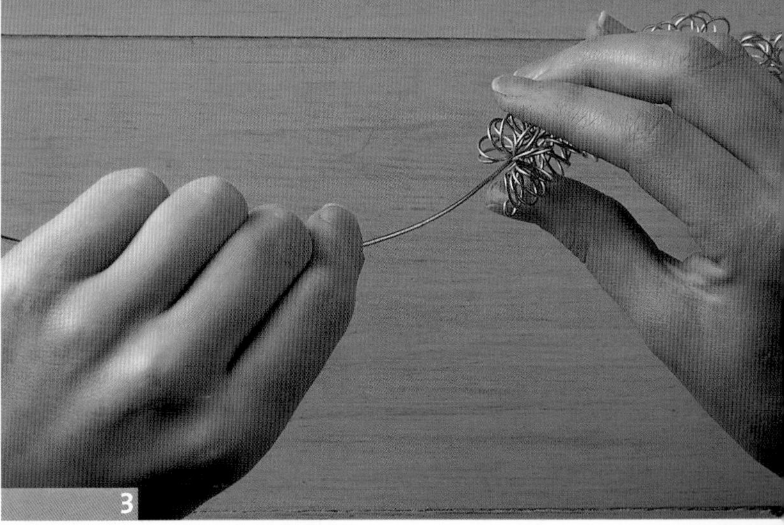

ELEGANT LANTERN

It is hard to believe that this unusual and elegant lantern has been made from plain old chicken wire. Chicken wire is a fantastic medium because it can be molded and sculpted into extraordinary shapes. Here, an elongated urn has been fashioned using pliers, and then hung from scrolled wire hooks suspended from the ceiling. A glass jar is wired securely inside to hold a small candle or night light. Glass beads threaded onto wire shimmer in the light.

MATERIALS

Chicken wire
Galvanized wire
Florist's wire
Glass jar
Approximately 400 glass beads
Earring head wires

TOOLS

Wire cutters
Round-nose pliers
Pliers

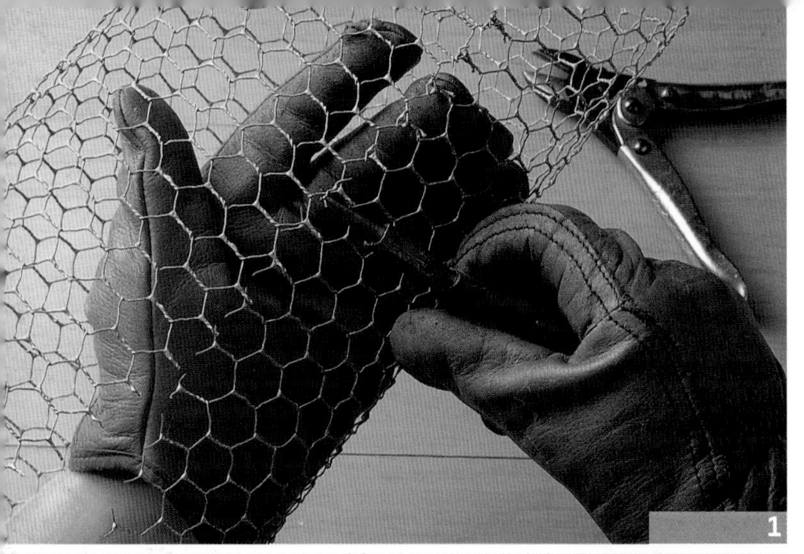

1

Cut a 16 x 20in (40 x 50cm) piece of chicken wire as shown, so that one side edge has two pronged wires projecting. Form the wire into a cylinder shape and wrap the projecting wires around the other side to secure.

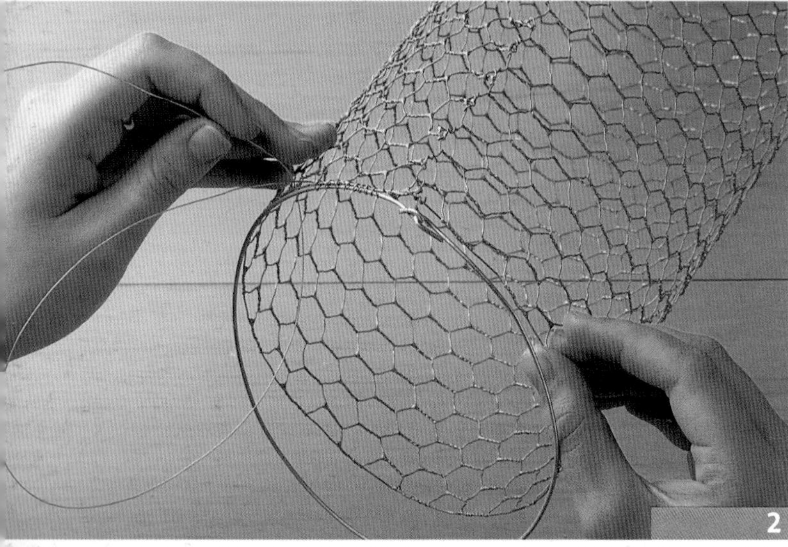

2

Cut a length of galvanized wire and wrap it around the top edge of the cylinder. Join the ends together by forming interlocking loops. Bind the circle to the top of your cylinder using florist's wire.

3

Using round-nose pliers, bend each horizontal strut on your netting into a V shape. This will create heart-shaped holes and make the wire less rigid and easier to manipulate. Shape the top of the cylinder into a gradually sloping neck by squeezing in the vertical struts to narrow the cylinder.

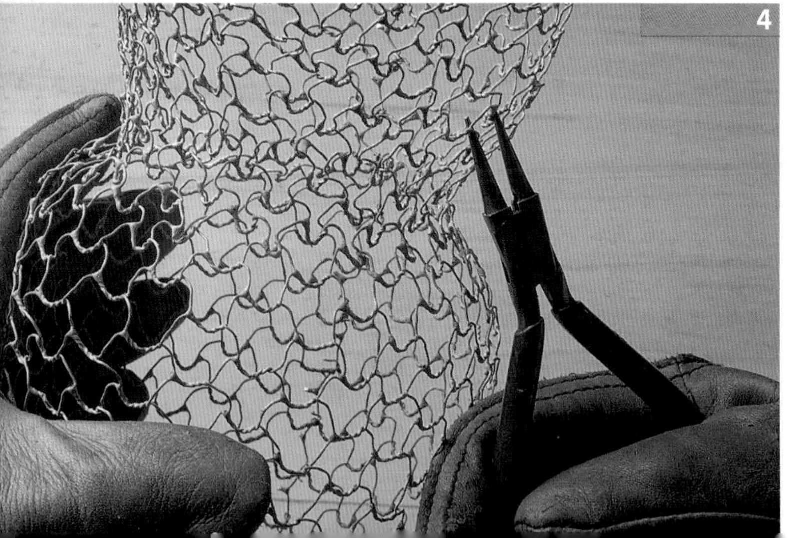

4

Once you have formed the neck, expand the wires in the sections above and below the neck to create a fuller "belly" by opening the pliers inside the wires to make them bigger and pulling outward.

5

Approximately halfway down your lantern, start to decrease the holes again to taper the shape into a "tail" at the bottom. Once you have formed the tail, compress it into a cone shape by using the pliers as shown.

6

Attach a wire from the tip of this tail and wrap it tightly round to form a 2in (4cm) long smooth cone. Attach the end to the mesh using jewelry pliers.

7

Cut four lengths of galvanized wire and form a small spiral on the end of each one using jewelry pliers. Loop each of these wires through the top rim of your lantern at quarter intervals and bend to shape. Bind them as shown, using florist's wire.

8

Wrap two lengths of wire in opposite directions around the neck of a glass jar that fits snugly into the neck of the lantern. Twist the wires together to form a secure fixture. Thread beads onto earring head wires, allowing sufficient wire to form a hanging loop and snipping off the excess. Hang a bead in each hole of the lantern that is large enough to do so from the shoulder of the lantern downward. Insert the glass jar and use the projecting wires to attach it to the neck of the lantern. To complete, wrap a length of wire around the neck to form a collar and thread each of the four hanging wires through a bead or similar, bend over to attach. Insert a looped wire through this to hang the lantern.

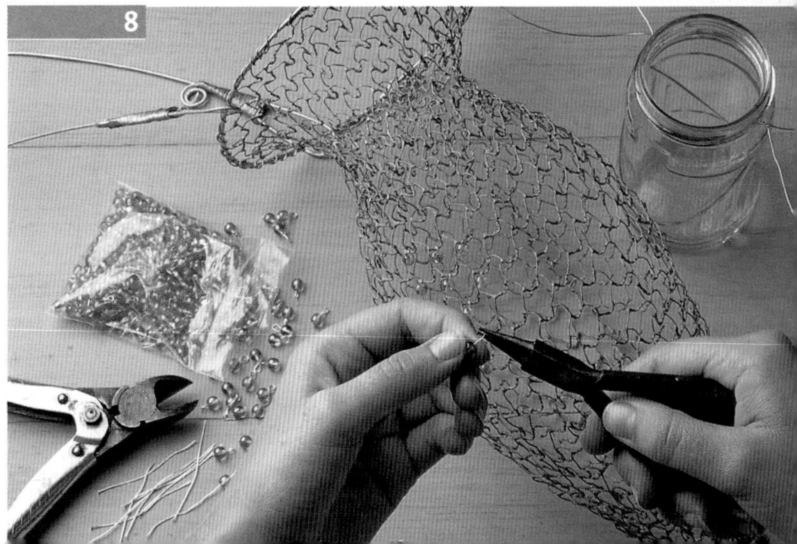

TABLE DECORATION

Create your own ornaments, table decorations, or objets d'art using wire for structure and glass for color and texture. Tripod and pyramid structures are stable and easy to create. Simply bend the wire to make feet, define their shape with beads, and join the wires together to form a top knot. Colored glass and beads can then be bound onto the structure for added decoration. Sea-washed glass (available in assorted colors and shapes from gift stores) and large recycled-glass beads have been used here for their beautiful color and texture, with small frosted seed beads woven into a mesh around the structure.

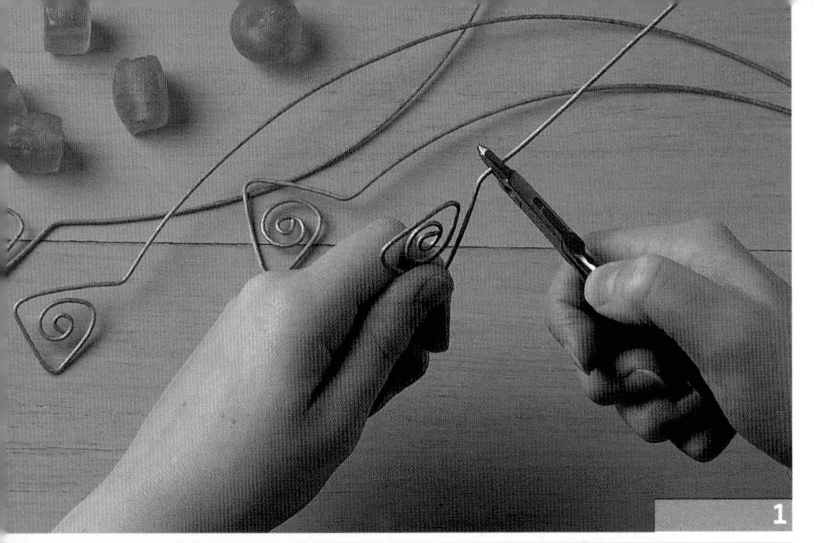

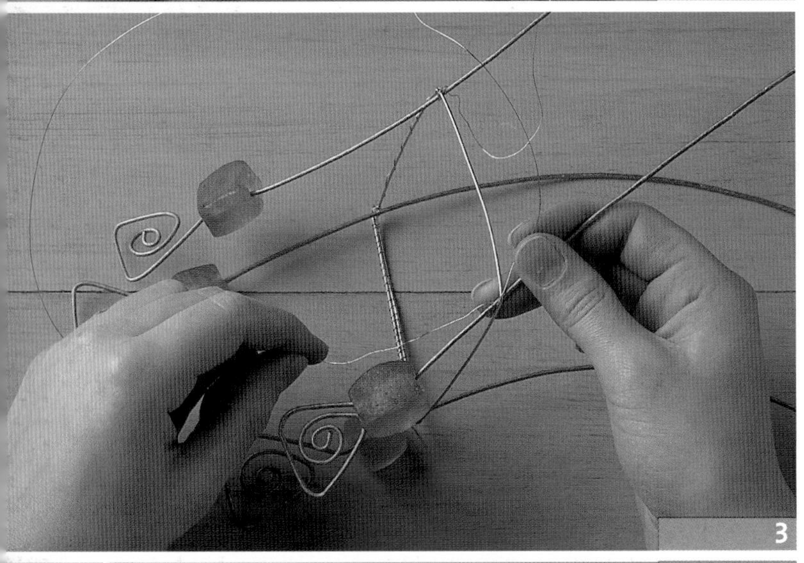

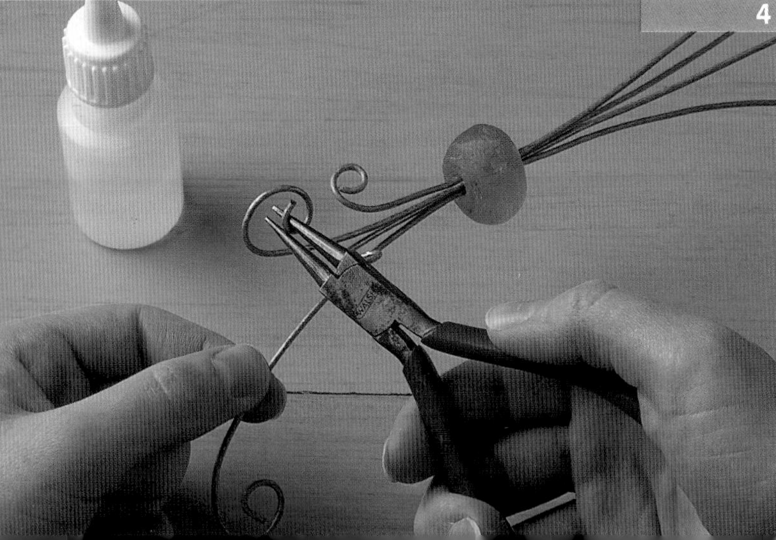

MATERIALS

1.5mm and 1.2mm galvanized wire
Fine binding wire
5 large frosted glass beads (one must have a hole big enough for all the wires to go through where they meet at the top)
Assortment of frosted glass seed beads

TOOLS

Wire cutters
Round-nose pliers
Household pliers

1

To make the frame, cut four lengths of 1.2mm wire and form a flat, open spiral at one end of each, using round-nose pliers. Use the pliers to bend the final curve of the spiral into a triangular shape to form a foot on the end of each length of wire.

2

Use household pliers to bend around 12in (30 cm) of 1.2mm wire into a square to form the base of the table decoration. Join the overlapping ends of the wire together using fine binding wire.

3

Thread a large glass bead onto each wire leg so that it sits just above the triangular foot. Secure each leg to the base frame with fine binding wire. Push the base frame down to the bottom of the four wire legs so that it sits just above the glass beads.

4

Gather together the four leg wires at the top and thread them through the remaining large bead. Using round-nose pliers, curl the end of each wire to make an attractive display.

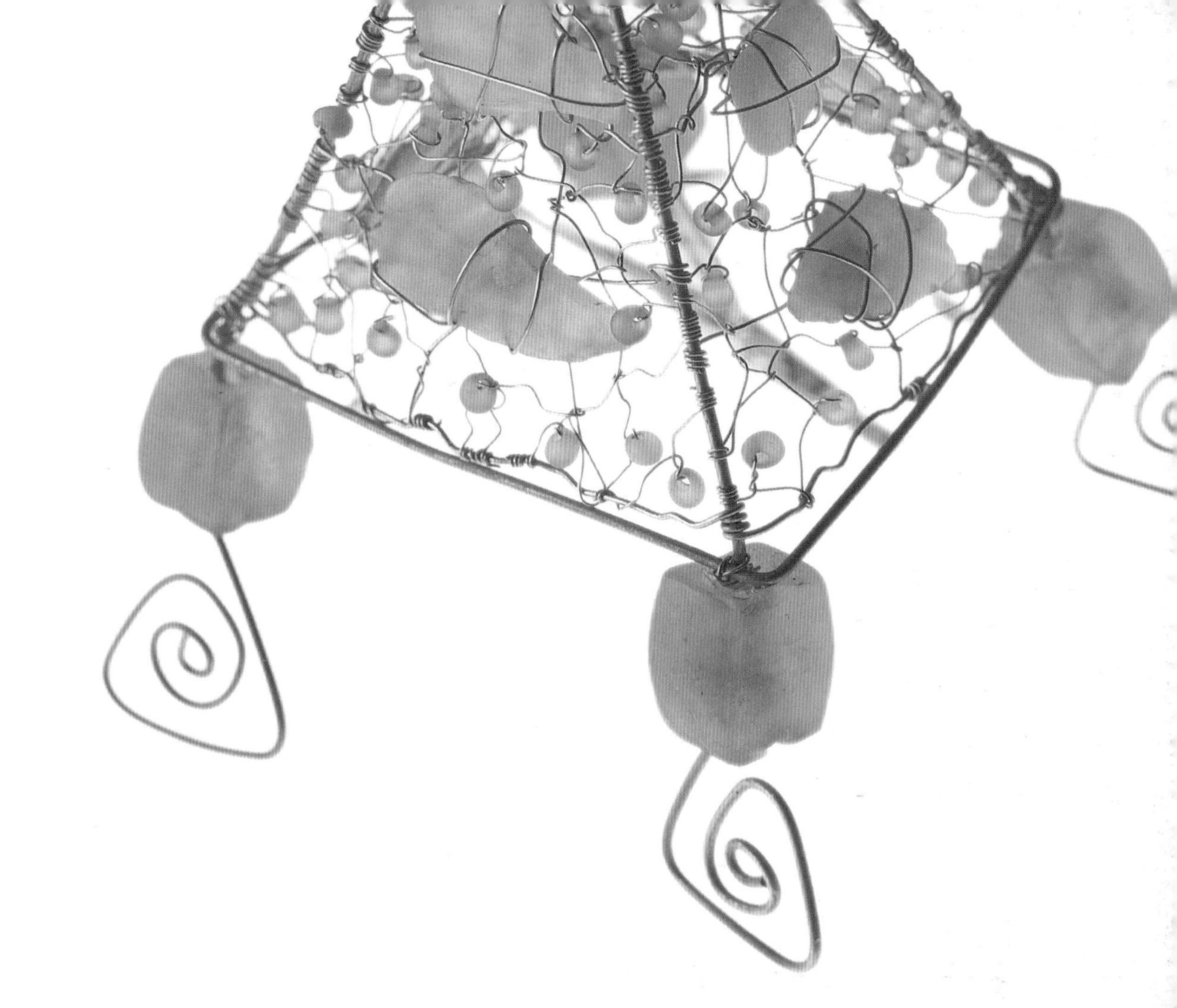

5

Bind pieces of sea-washed glass to the frame using 1.5mm wire. Three pieces of glass were bound to each side in this example, but you can vary the number depending on the size of your structure.

6

Thread seed beads onto fine binding wire, twisting the wire at the base of each bead to hold it in position. Bind the wire randomly around the structure to form a delicately beaded mesh.

5

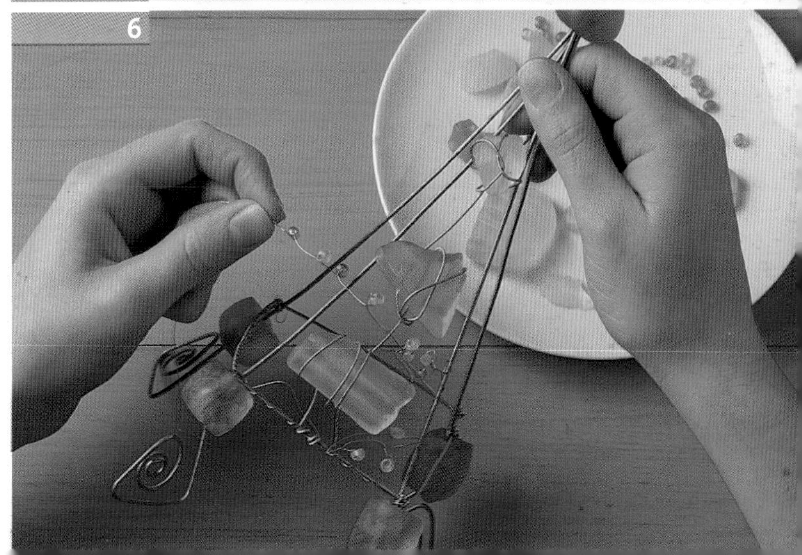
6

GLASS CARRIER

This pretty wire carrier allows you to transport glasses safely to the garden on a summer's day. It is made from sturdy wire but with a delicate design. The wiggly wire is easily made with a simple gig (see Basic Techniques, page 15, to find out how to make one). Moroccan tea glasses have been chosen because of their color and decoration, but other glasses would work equally well. You can adapt the design so that it accommodates more glasses if necessary.

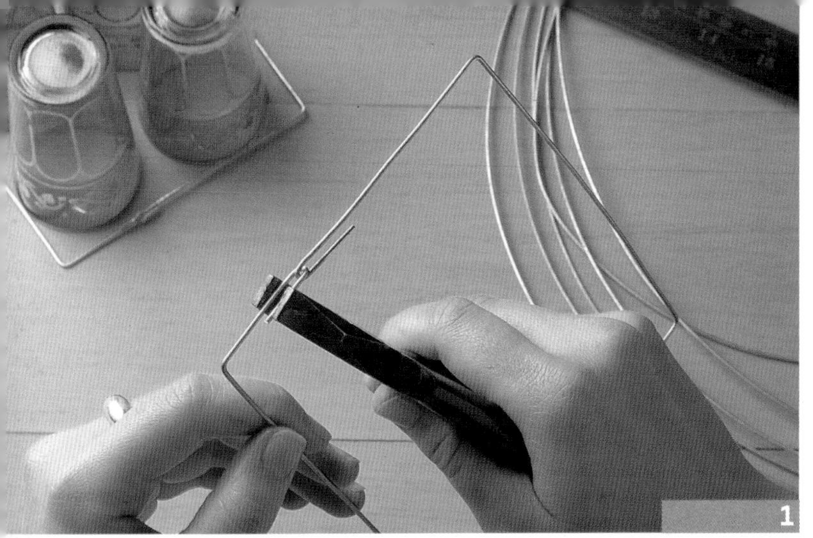

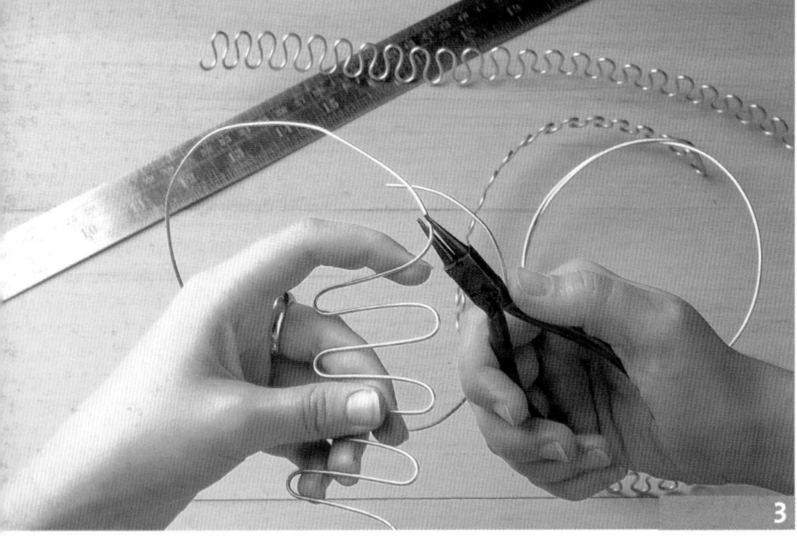

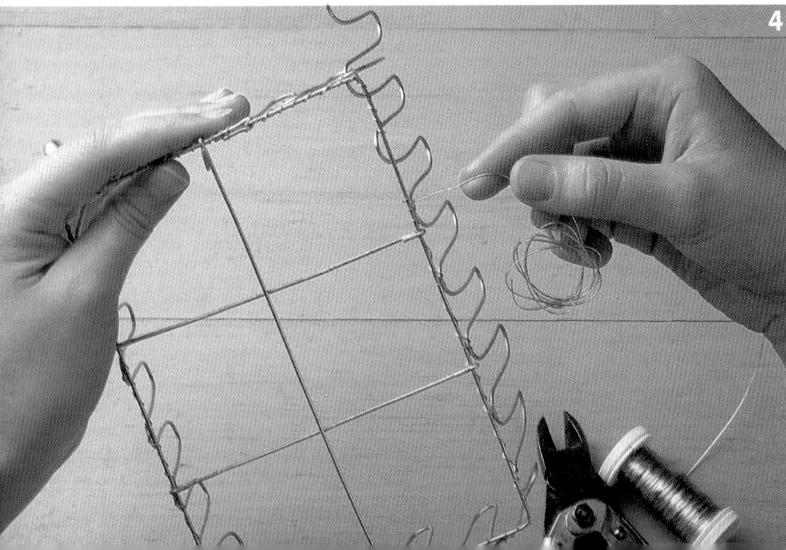

MATERIALS

Six small glasses
1.2mm galvanized garden wire
Florist's wire

TOOLS

Paper, pencil, and ruler
Wire cutters
Household pliers
Jewelry pliers
Simple gig

1

Arrange the glasses on a sheet of paper and use a pencil and ruler to draw a rectangle around them at their widest points. Cut a length of galvanized wire long enough to form into the required rectangle, allowing 3/4in (2cm) excess all around. Mark the corner points on the wire and use household pliers to bend each one to form a 90-degree angle. Form a loop at each end of the wire, interlock them, and squeeze them closed. This forms the base of the carrier. Repeat to make a rectangle for the top edge.

2

Cut four lengths of galvanized wire to fit lengthwise across the base rectangle and four to fit across it widthwise, allowing 3/4in (2cm) excess on each piece. Space these evenly across the rectangle and attach them by bending the ends around the base frame with pliers. Repeat for the top frame but use only one wire divider lengthwise and two widthwise. This will create six spaces for the glasses.

3

Use round-nose pliers to form a length of curved wire about 2 1/2in (6cm) wide and long enough to wrap around the frame (see Basic Techniques, page 15). Add a length of wiggly wire 3/4 (2cm) deep, made on a gig (see

Basic Techniques, page 15) long enough to wrap around your base with enough left over to make a handle.

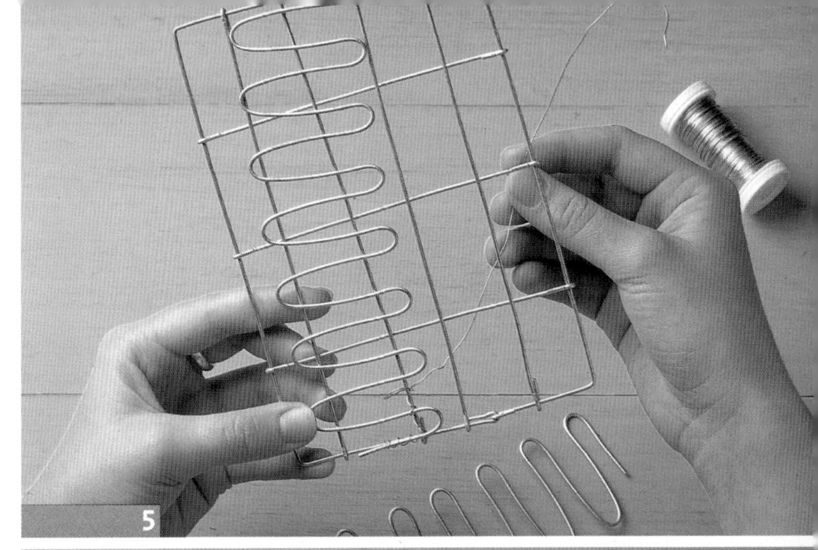

4

Using florist wire, bind the deeper wiggly wire to the top framework, bending it to fit around the corners.

5

Make two lengths of wiggly wire to fit across your base frame as shown and bond into place.

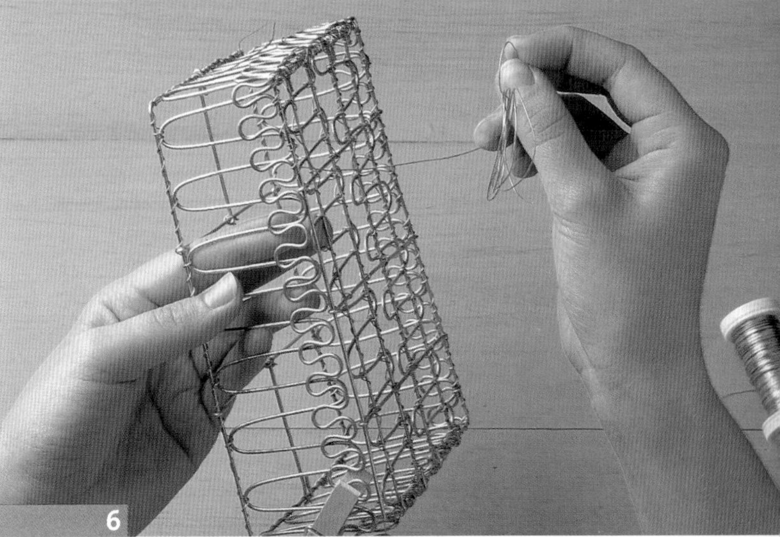

6

Position small wiggly wire around the base edge of the sides, then place bottom frame in position and bind these together along the edge.

7

Make the handle by binding two lengths of wire to either side of a length of narrow wiggly wire. Bend this at a 90-degree angle at each end to form the handle shape.

8

Bind the handle onto the carrier in a central position. make decorative spirals with the excess handle wire using jewelry pliers.

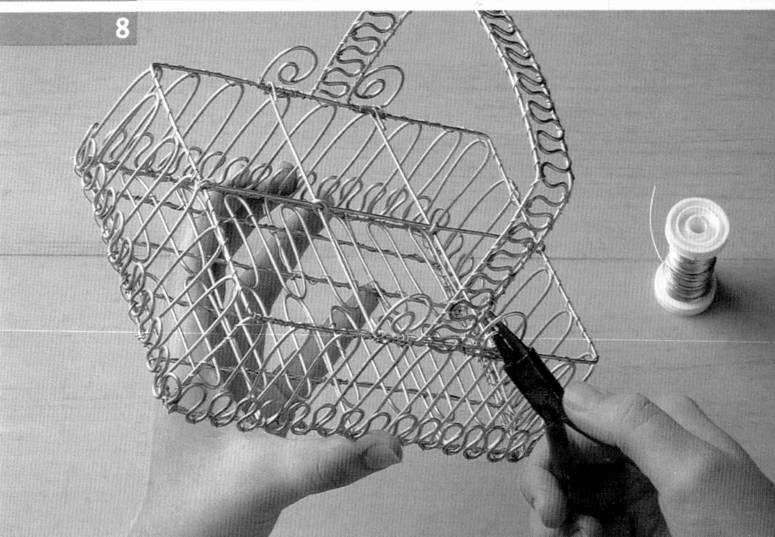

MAGAZINE RACK

Metal grating has a certain industrial chic that, when married with plastic tubing, iridescent marbles, pearls, and beads, produces a stylish design with novelty and elegance. Metal grating is available from garden centers and is easy to work with, though you may wish to wear gloves to protect your hands from scratches. Thick wire threaded through plastic tubing gives substance to the legs of the rack and holds large marbles that are heavy enough to anchor the structure. The grating can be colored using metallic spray paint.

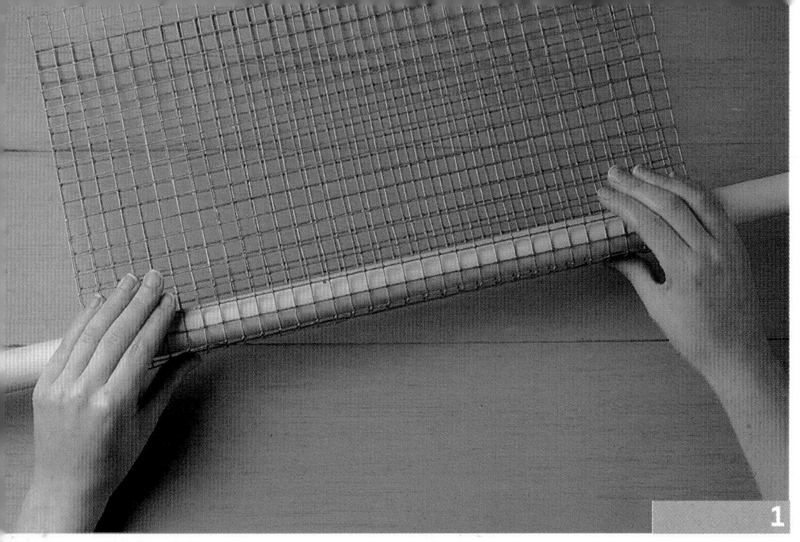

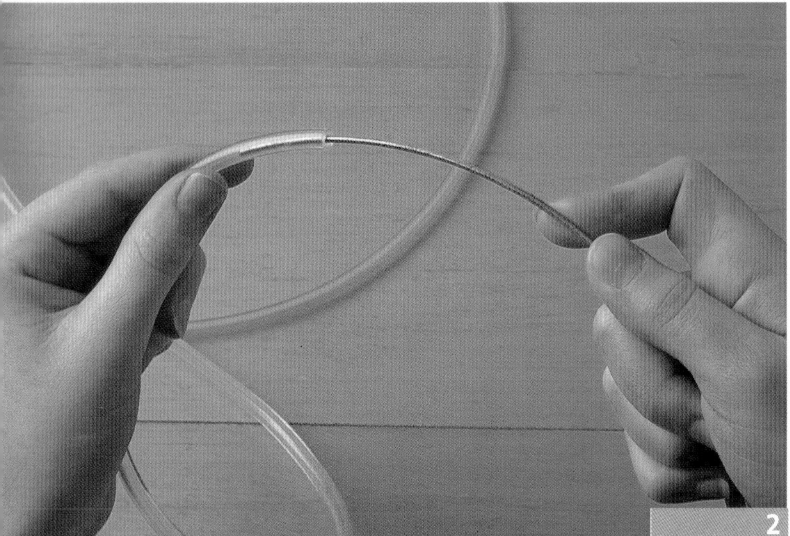

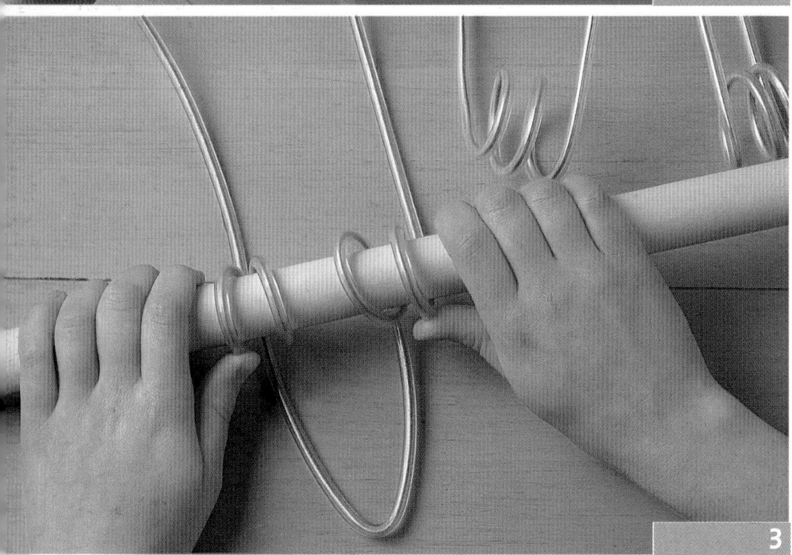

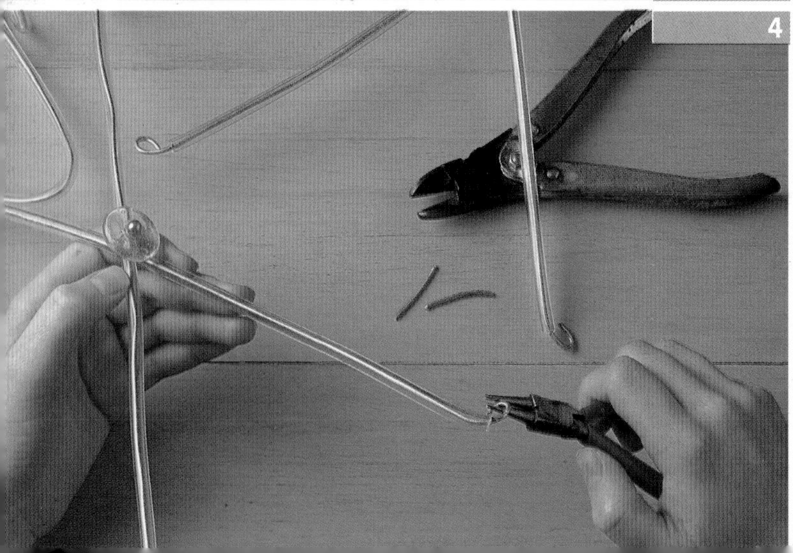

MATERIALS

Galvanized metal grating with 1/4in (6mm) grid
Spray paint (optional)
10ft (3m) plastic tubing (6mm diameter)
2.5mm galvanized wire
Fine binding wire
Glass disk beads
Pearl beads
4 large marbles
Strong glue

TOOLS

Wire cutters
Metal file
Long piece of thick dowel
Round-nose pliers
Chain-nose (snipe-nose) pliers

1

Cut out a rectangle of wire grating with wire cutters. The size of the grating will depend on the size of magazine rack you require. File the edges until smooth. Spray paint if desired and allow to dry. Bend the grating in half around a piece of dowel.

2

Cut two 5ft (1.5m) lengths of plastic tubing. Thread a length of 2.5mm wire through the center of each tube, leaving around 1in (2.5cm) excess wire at each end. Bend both wire tubes in the middle to form V shapes.

3

Measure 4 1/2in (12cm) from the bottom of the V shape, then wrap each arm three times around the dowel to produce a pair of short coils, as shown. When you have finished, the arms of the V shape should point in the same direction as the base of the V. The coils will form the feet of the magazine rack.

4

Cross the arms of each V shape and secure in the center with binding wire. Decorate both joins by threading a disk bead and a pearl bead onto the binding wire and attach securely. Use round-nose pliers to form the four ends of the wire arms into loops.

5

Click a large marble into each coiled wire foot of the magazine rack. If necessary, put some strong glue on the underside of each marble and allow it to dry securely in place.

6

Make a decorative edging along the top of both sides of the grating by binding disk and pearl beads along them, as shown.

7

Attach the grating to the legs by slightly bending the inverted V of each leg inward and binding it to the base of the grating about five squares in from the edge, as shown.

8

Hook the looped ends of the legs through the top edge of the grating and squeeze the loop firmly closed with chain-nose (snipe-nose) pliers. The structure should now be stable.

5

6

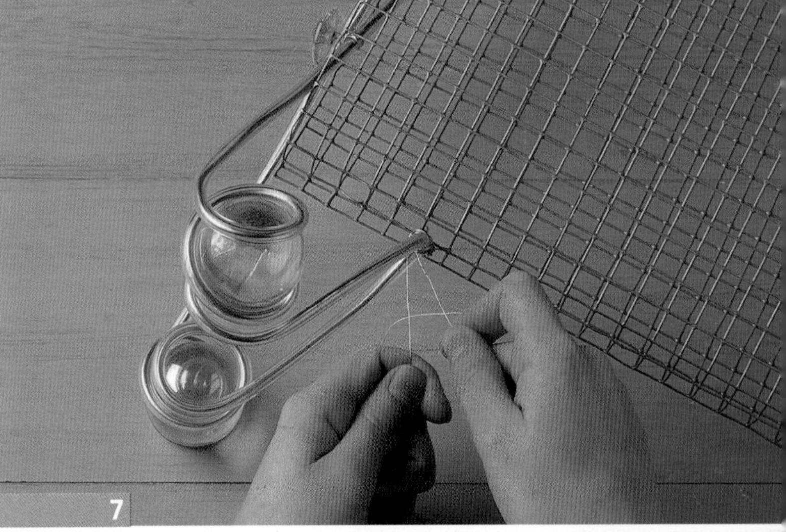
7

8

TEA GLASSES

Simple, inexpensive drinking glasses have been transformed into beautiful tea glasses by the addition of an elegant wire holder, making them ideal for fruit teas, mulled wine, or hot toddies. The flat shape of the wire surround is achieved by hammering galvanized wire. This is a simple technique that produces unusual and stylish results. For a more elaborate effect, try using colored glass and hammered copper wire.

1

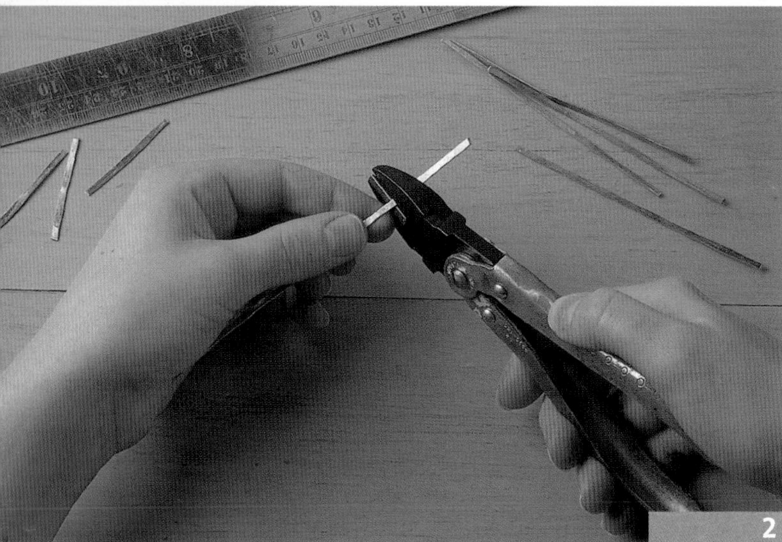

2

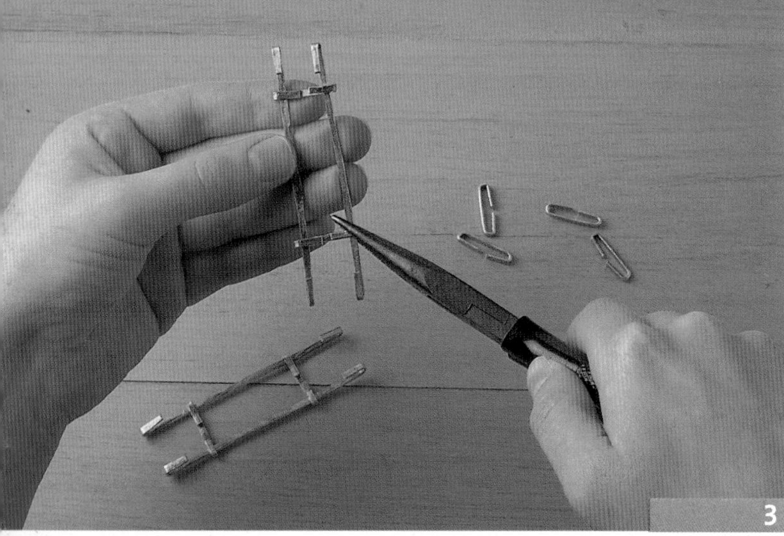

3

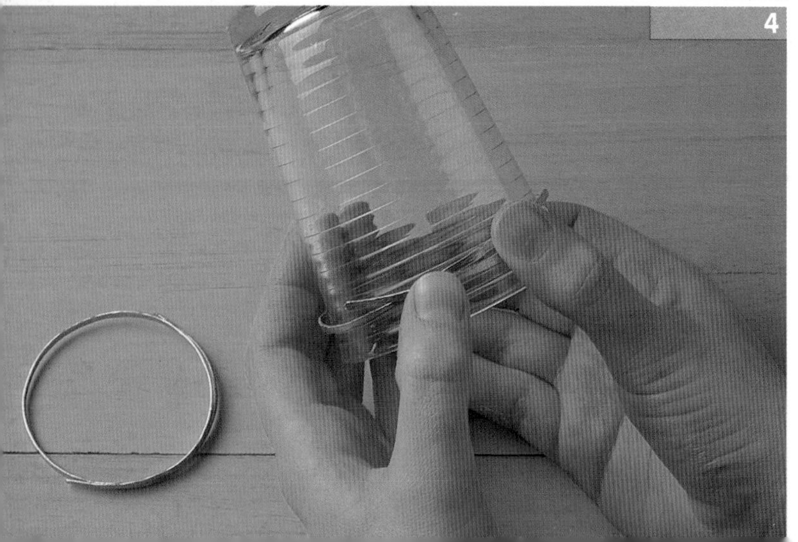

4

MATERIALS

2.5mm galvanized wire

Glasses

TOOLS

Sheet of metal (to hammer onto)

Hammer

Wire cutters

Chain-nose (snipe-nose) pliers

1

Place the sheet of metal on a sturdy surface and hammer along the length of the wire until it is sufficiently flat. It is best to do this in small sections because it is easier than handling long lengths of wire.

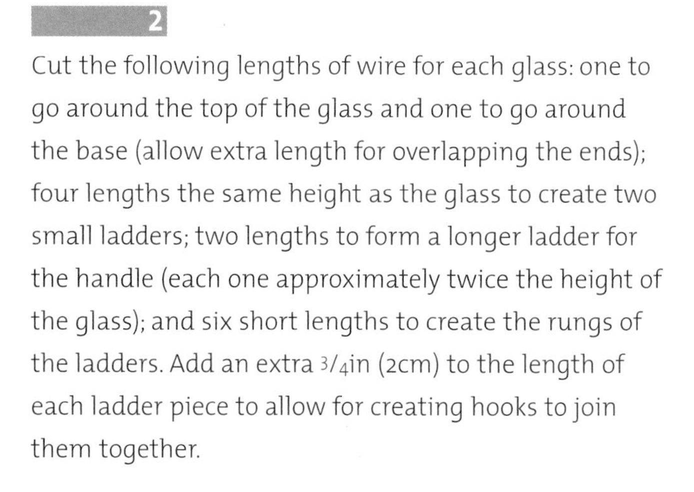

2

Cut the following lengths of wire for each glass: one to go around the top of the glass and one to go around the base (allow extra length for overlapping the ends); four lengths the same height as the glass to create two small ladders; two lengths to form a longer ladder for the handle (each one approximately twice the height of the glass); and six short lengths to create the rungs of the ladders. Add an extra 3/4in (2cm) to the length of each ladder piece to allow for creating hooks to join them together.

3

First, assemble two small ladders, using the four glass-height lengths of wire and four of the short pieces of wire. Use chain-nose pliers to bend a small hook at each end of the longer wires, then use two short pieces of wire to join pairs of the longer wires together to form a small ladder. Use pliers to bend the ends of the short wires securely around the longer wires.

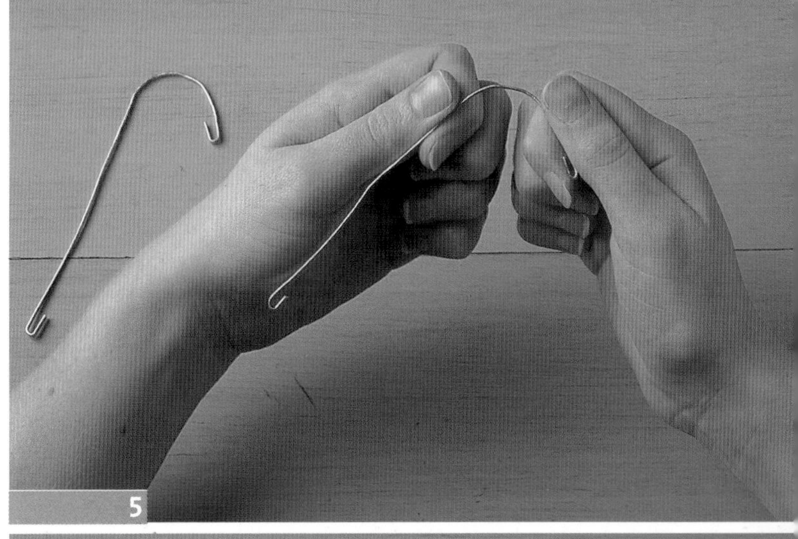

4

Make two circles of wire, one for the top of the glass and one for the bottom. Leave the excess wire in place because they will be cut later.

5

Use pliers to bend a small hook at each end of the handle wires, then use your fingers to form the wires into the desired shape. Make sure that both pieces are the same and join them together in the same way as the ladders in step 3.

6

Using the glass to gauge the size, attach the top band of the glass holder to the handle by threading the ends of the band through the hooks of the handle. Use pliers to bend the ends back over the handle hooks to secure.

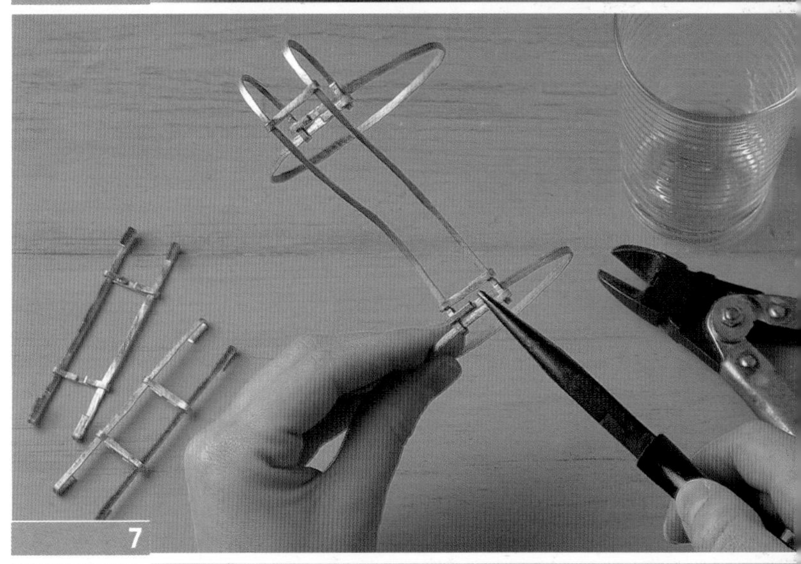

7

Attach the bottom of the handle in the same way, then cut off the excess wire from both the top and bottom bands. Use pliers to squeeze the ends firmly to create a secure fixing.

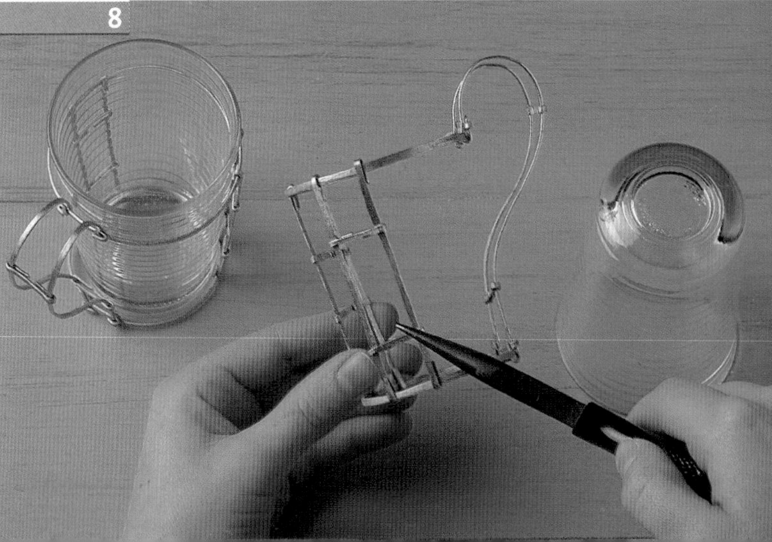

8

Attach the two ladders to the top and bottom band in the same way. Make sure the ladders are evenly spaced and that the ends are well squeezed together.

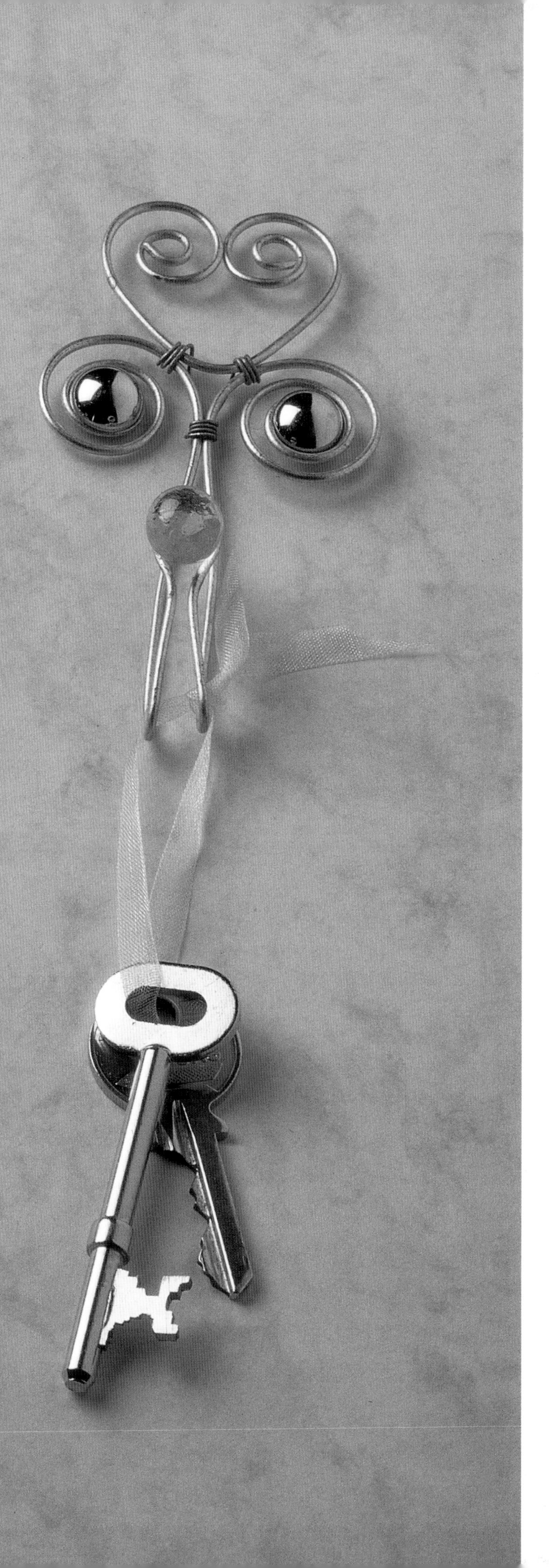

WALL HOOKS

These wall hooks are both decorative and functional. They are quick and easy to make, so this project is ideal for beginners—all you need is some galvanized wire and a pair of round-nose pliers to form these attractive shapes. When attaching the hooks to the wall, use screws with a decorative head for best effect. If you wish, you can adapt the design to make a hanging rack by binding a row of hooks to a wire frame.

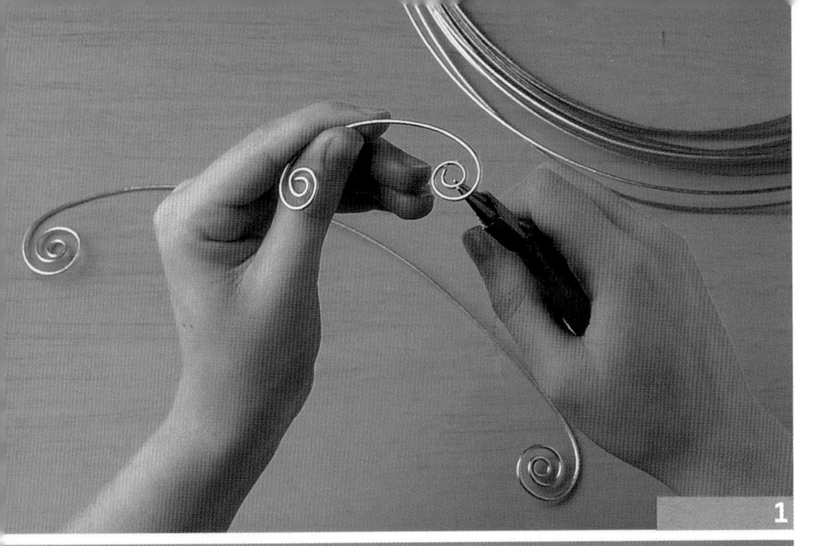

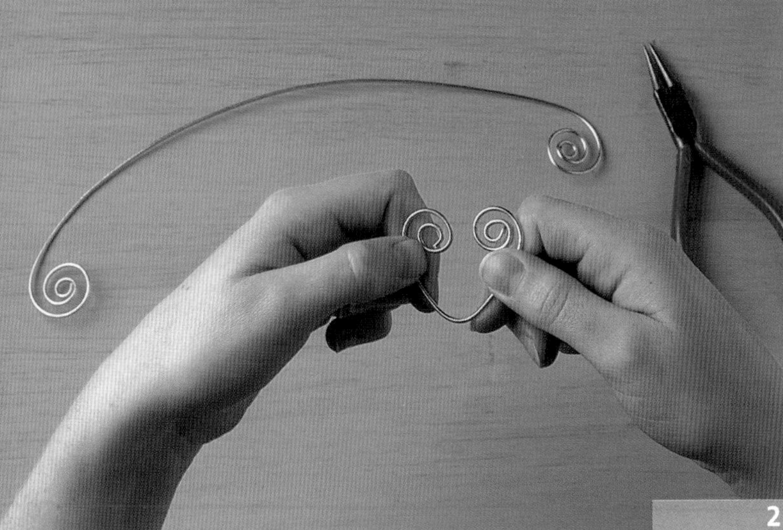

MATERIALS

1.6mm galvanized wire
Fine binding wire
Strong glue
Small glass marbles (1 per hook)
Screws (2 per hook)

TOOLS

Wire cutters
Round-nose pliers
Pencil

1

Cut a 20in (50cm) and an 8in (20cm) length of wire. Use round-nose pliers to shape both lengths of wire into double-ended spirals (see Basic Techniques, page 13).

2

Holding the shorter wire in both hands, place a finger midway along the section of wire and bend the spirals toward each other to form a heart (see Basic Techniques, page 13).

3

Find the midpoint of the longer wire, and using pliers, create a small loop by bending the wire around the pliers, as shown.

4

Place the fingers of both hands between the arms of the wire V shape and press your thumbs just beneath the spirals to bend the wire inward. The fingers will resist the bend, causing the two arms of the V shape to bow out slightly.

5

Place a pencil across the wire approximately 1in (2.5cm) up from the bottom loop and bend the wire around the pencil to form a hook.

6

Use fine binding wire to join the two long arms of the hook together just beneath the pair of spirals. Then attach the heart shape to the hook section by wrapping binding wire around the top of each spiral and the base of the heart, as shown. Use strong glue to attach a marble to the loop at the end of the hook. Attach the hook to the wall by inserting a screw through the center of each of the larger spirals.

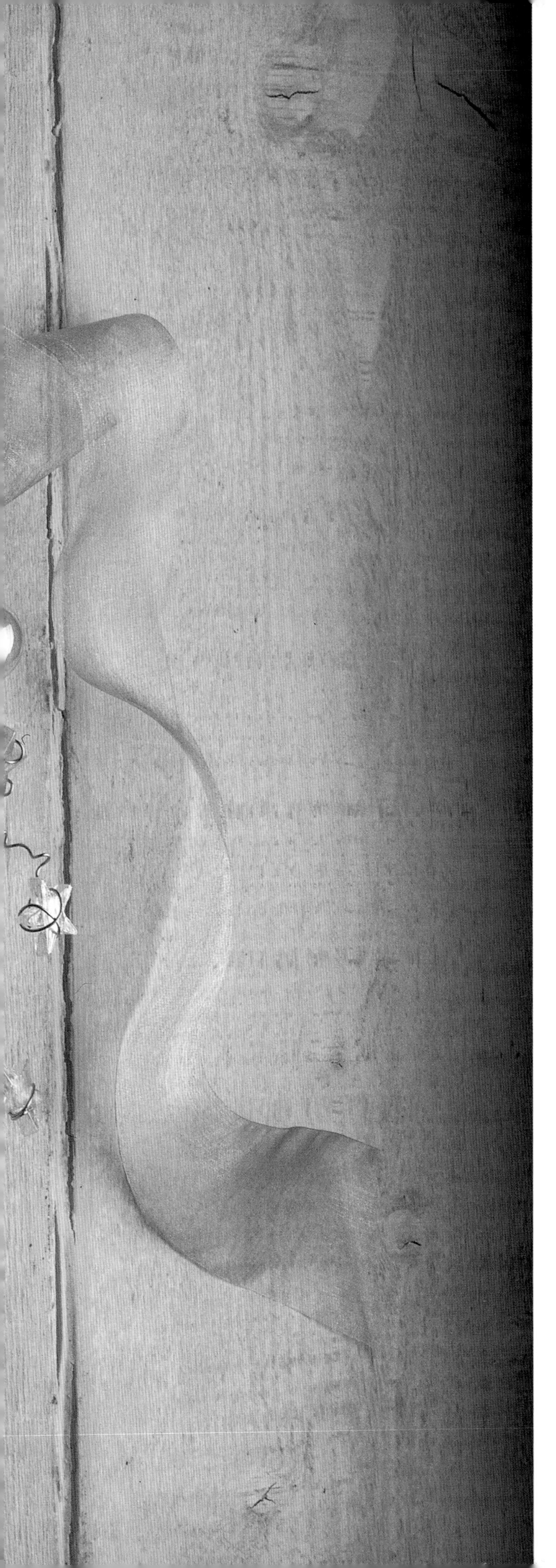

WIRE WREATH

This lovely wreath made from interconnecting spirals of coiled wire is the perfect winter wonderland decoration for Christmas festivities. Wire springs randomly shoot out glass stars, and iridescent Christmas baubles are securely suspended within the wire loops. A sparkling ribbon adds to the exuberance. Hang the wreath on a door in deep midwinter and let the snow and frost complete the effect.

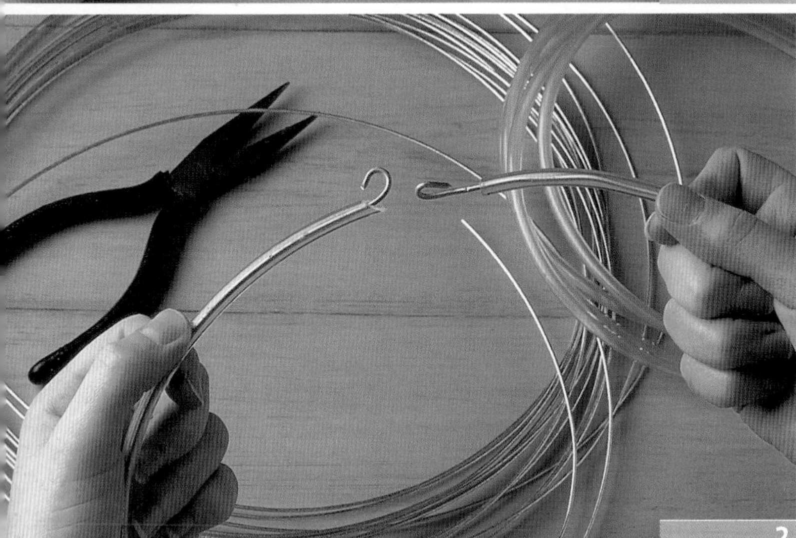

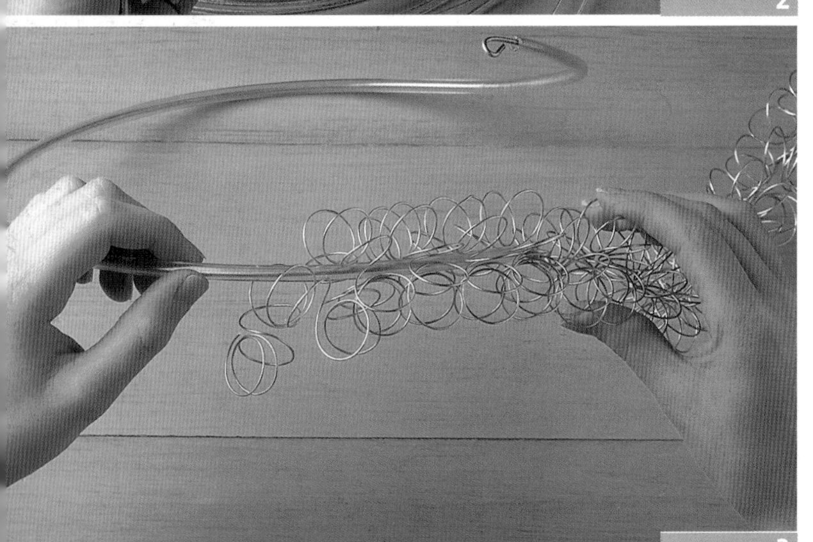

MATERIALS

0.9mm and 1mm galvanized wire
32in (80cm) plastic tubing
Glass stars
Strong glue
Small glass Christmas baubles on wires
Ribbon

TOOLS

1/8in (4mm) and 3/4in (2cm) dowel
Wire cutters
Round-nose pliers

1

Make two coiled spirals using 0.9mm galvanized wire (see Basic Techniques, page 17). Use the narrow dowel to make one of the spirals and the thick dowel to make the other. Make another coil of the same length using the narrow dowel but only go as far as step 1 in the Basic Techniques. Use your fingers to stretch the coil into an extended spring; do not bend the coils in the way that you would to form a coiled spiral.

2

Thread 1mm galvanized wire through a 32in (80cm) length of plastic tubing. Use pliers to form a loop at each end of the wire, as shown.

3

Carefully thread the wire tubing through the center of the larger coiled spiral. If this is difficult, you may prefer to wrap the coil spirally around the tubing.

4

Form the wire tubing into a circle and join the interlocking loops together. Squeeze the loops closed with round-nose pliers.

5

5

Cut the extended spring into 5in (13cm) lengths. Wrap one end of each length around a small glass star. Use pliers to make sure they are held securely, and glue them if necessary.

6

6

Embed the smaller coiled spiral within the wire loops of the wreath by pushing it in so that it is held between the larger loops.

7

7

Attach the stars randomly around the wreath. Use the ends of the wires holding the stars to secure the smaller coiled spiral in place by binding the wires around both the spirals and the wreath's core.

8

8

Bind Christmas baubles randomly around the wreath. These should fit snugly between the larger loops, with their wire ends entwined around the wreath's core. Add a decorative bow to the top, binding it in place with some wire.

WINDOW SCREEN

When light shines through this window screen, beautiful colored patterns are reflected into the room through the pretty glass beads. Make sure you measure the window frame accurately before you start, and work out the pattern of the beads using colored pencils and graph paper. Choose beads that look good when held up to the light. Make sure that all the elements are secure before fixing the screen to the window frame using screws through the corner loops.

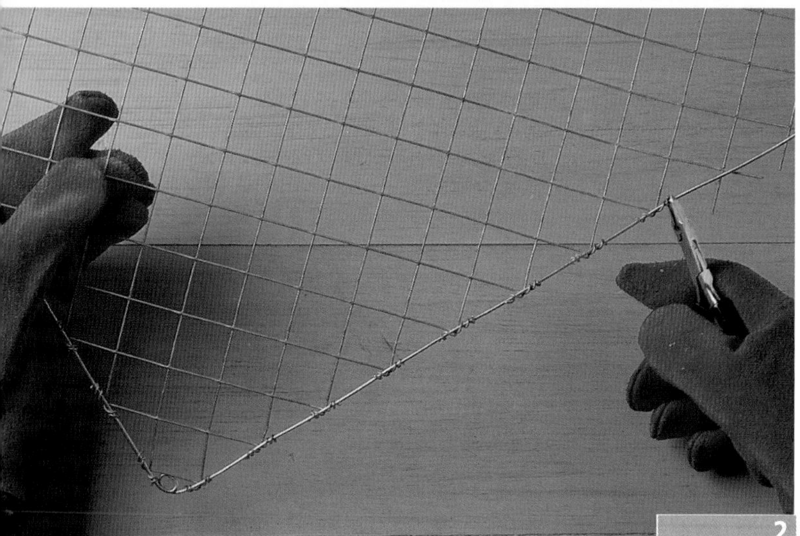

MATERIALS

Galvanized metal grating with 1in (2.5cm) grid
1.5mm galvanized wire
Frosted glass star
Fine binding wire
Frosted glass beads in various sizes
Frosted glass droplets
Strong glue
Four screws

TOOLS

Wire cutters
Round-nose pliers
Miricle pliers
Graph paper and colored pencils

1

Measure the window frame where you are going to hang the screen; double-check to make sure you have done so accurately. Carefully cut the metal grating with wire cutters to the correct size; it should fit comfortably into the space. Cut a length of galvanized wire long enough to go all the way around the edge of the grating with a little extra for the corner loops. Use round-nose pliers to form the corner loops, as shown.

2

Bind the wire frame around the grating by bending the cut edges of the grating around the frame using miricle pliers. Make sure it is secure and that all the wire ends are firmly bent around the frame.

3

Work out the center point of the grating and cut out a section large enough for the star to fit in.

4

Suspend the star in the hole by using fine binding wire to attach it securely to the surrounding grating.

5

Attach the beads to the grating according to the pattern you wish to create; it is best if you design it on graph paper first using colored pencils that match the different colors of the beads you are using. Here, one bead is suspended per square to form a diamond pattern on the screen. To suspend the beads, use a doubled length of fine binding wire. Wrap each strand of the wire around a corner of the square, thread both strands through the bead, then separate the strands again and wrap them around the opposite corners. This will suspend the bead in the center of the square.

6

Position the glass droplets as desired, binding them into place and neatly tying the binding wires at the back of the screen. Secure them with some strong glue if necessary. Screw the finished screen into place on the window frame.

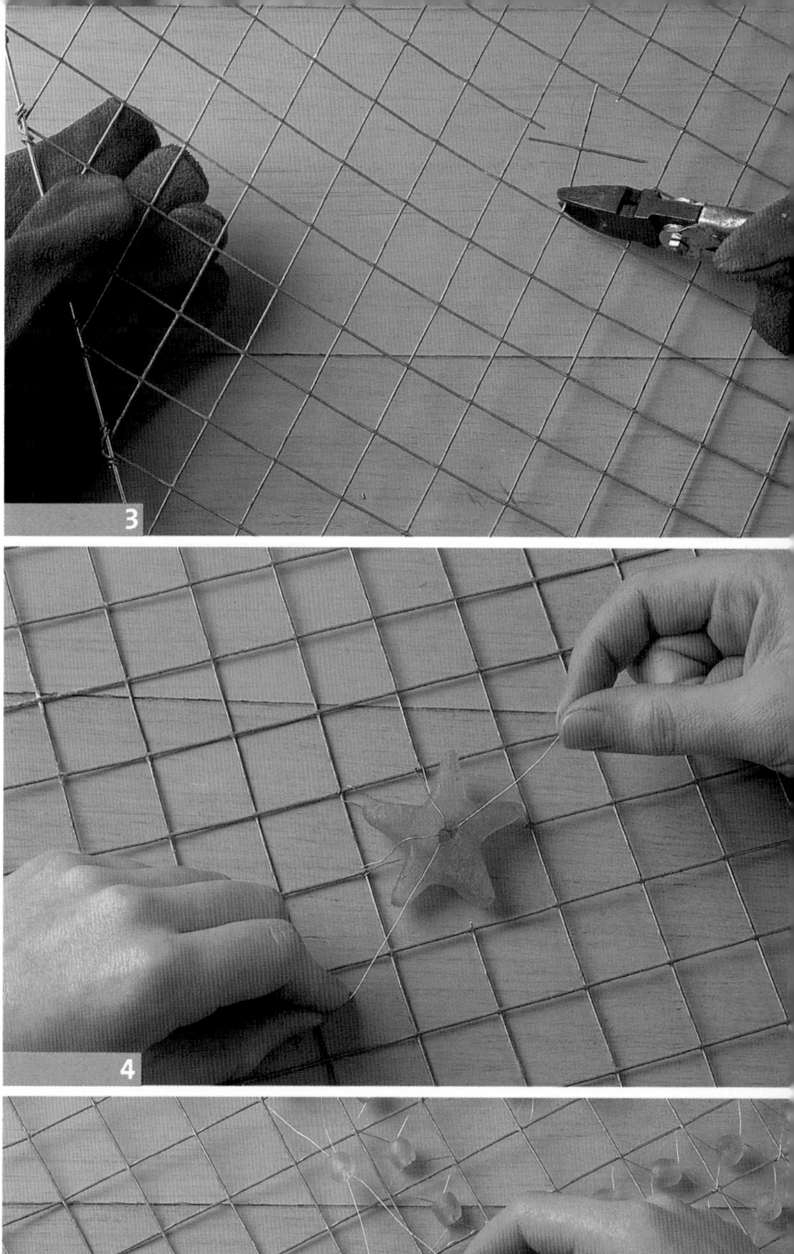

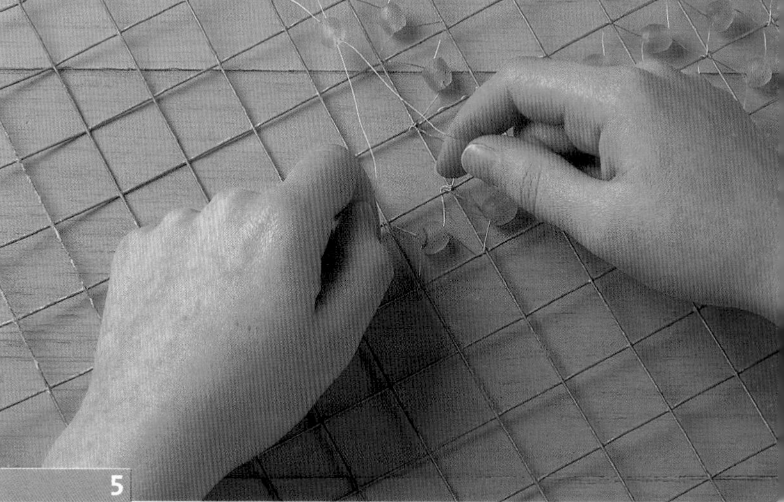

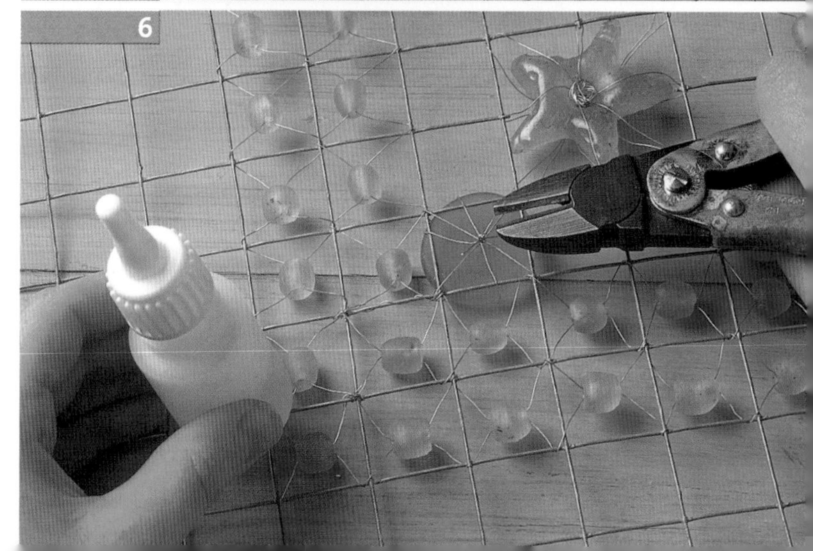

BEADED BOWL

Beaded wire has been fashioned into a lace-effect pattern to transform this plain glass bowl into a delicate centerpiece, perfect for a summer party. Cone-shaped beads are used for the feet because of their flat bottoms, but other shapes could be substituted if you prefer. Make sure the wires do not protrude from the base of the feet or they will scratch the surface of the table. Remember, too, that the bigger the bowl, the longer the beaded wire must be.

MATERIALS

Glass bowl
0.6mm galvanized wire
Frosted glass seed beads
Frosted glass round beads
Frosted glass cone-shaped beads
Strong glue

TOOLS

Wire cutters
Round-nose pliers

1

Choose the bowl you wish to decorate with beaded wire. Thread seed beads onto a long piece of wire, leaving some wire unbeaded at the end to allow the beads to move when you bend the wire into shape. Count the number of beads required to make a petal shape; this will depend on how large you want the petals to be. Starting with a petal, form the top edging of the bowl by looping and twisting the beaded wire to form petals at regular intervals. This example has 22 beads per petal, 8 beads between each petal, and 20 petals in total.

2

Once you have sufficient edging to surround the top of the bowl, cut off any excess wire and use pliers to form a small loop at the end. Link this around the base of the first petal and squeeze closed.

3

Thread beads onto another length of wire to form the scallops between every alternate petal. Count the number of beads required to make each scallop; this example has 24 beads per scallop. Make a space between the beads at the end of each scallop and twist the wire around the neck of the petals to connect them.

4

Form a circle of beaded wire to fit around the base of the bowl. Use pliers to form a small loop at each end of the wire and link them together, squeezing the loops closed to secure.

5

Cut lengths of wire to make the side struts of the bowl; you will need one strut per scallop. Cut the wires 1in (2.5cm) longer than the depth of the bowl measured from the center of the scallops to the bottom ring of beads. Use pliers to form a small loop at one end of each wire. Thread a round frosted bead onto each wire, then enough seed beads to reach to the bottom ring.

6

Hook the top loop of each wire strut onto the center of a scallop, then squeeze the loop closed with pliers. Bend the other end of each strut slightly to keep the beads from falling off.

7

Loop the end wires of each strut around the beaded base ring at regular intervals. You should be left with some unbeaded wire projecting below the base ring for each strut.

8

Thread an equal number of seed beads onto each of these wires to make the feet; two beads per foot in this example. Trim the excess wire, leaving just enough wire to slide a conical foot bead onto the end. Make sure no wire protrudes through the cone beads or they will scratch the surface where you place the bowl. When you are satisfied, use strong glue to attach the cone beads securely in place. Put the glass bowl inside the beaded frame and arrange the petals decoratively.

5

6

7

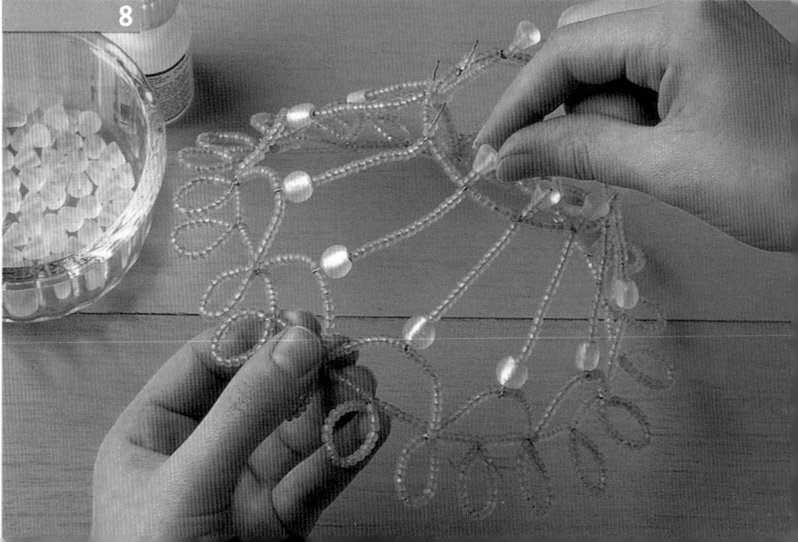
8

EVENING PURSE

It is hard to believe that this glittering purse is made from wire. Once knitted, the wire becomes surprisingly soft and tactile. The ends of the wires are woven into the knitting and used to bind the back and front together, so there are no loose ends. It is lined with purple velvet, making it suitable for carrying light items such as lipstick. This bag has been made in rich reds and purples, but you could use other colors if you prefer.

MATERIALS

Enameled copper wire in red, crimson, violet, wine, and purple
Approximately 440 red beads
Approximately 960 beads in autumnal colors
Purple velvet
Needle and thread
Snap fastener (press stud)
Cord for handle
Tassel and bead

TOOLS

3mm and 4mm knitting needles
Scissors

1

Thread 440 beads onto the red wire, 202 beads onto the crimson wire, 132 beads onto the violet wire, 78 beads onto the wine-colored wire, and 108 beads onto the purple wire. Use red beads on the red wire and autumnal colors on the other wires. Add a few extra beads to each wire to allow for errors.

2

Follow the pattern, keeping the stitch gauge (tension) as even as possible. To work beads into a stitch, draw a bead up the wire to the front of the work, knit the following stitch, then draw up another bead to the front of the work and knit the next stitch, and so on.

3

Join in new colors as when knitting with yarn or cut the old color leaving a short length that you can twist together with the new color close to the knitting.

4

To get the perfect finished shape, gently squeeze the wire at the edges, using either your fingers or pliers. Make sure all loose ends are worked in at this stage.

5

With wrong sides together, join the front and back pieces of the bag using matching wire. Make sure you join the lengths of wire securely, then oversew the seams.

6

Use the knitted bag as a template to cut two pieces of velvet lining. With right sides together, sew around the bottom edges using backstitch.

7

Turn the lining bag right side out and place inside the knitted bag. Turn over the top unbeaded edge of the wire bag and oversew it to the lining.

8

Sew on the snap fastener, cord handle, bead and tassel.

PATTERN

Cast on 44 stitches using 3mm needles and red wire. Knit 5 rows with no beads. Knit 10 rows with a bead between each stitch. Change to 4mm needles and crimson wire. Knit 1 row with no beads. On next and every alternate row, add a bead in each stitch; decrease 1 stitch at each end of next and every following 4th row until there are 38 stitches (10 rows). Change to violet wire. Knit 1 row with no beads. On next and every alternate row, add a bead in each stitch; decrease 1 stitch at each end of next and every alternate row until there are 30 stitches (8 rows). Change to wine-colored wire. Knit 1 row with no beads. On next and every alternate row, add a bead in each stitch; decrease 1 stitch at each end of next and every alternate row until there are 24 stitches (6 rows). Change to purple wire. Knit 1 row with no beads. On next and every alternate row, add a bead in each stitch; decrease 1 stitch at each end of next and every alternative row until 1 stitch remains. Bind off (cast off). Repeat pattern for the back of the bag without beads.

RADIANT MIRROR

This wonderful surround, made from galvanized wire and a selection of pretty beads, transforms a plain mirror into a thing of beauty. Frosted glass beads have been used here to complement the glass. Small triangular edging beads are perfect for the borders. You can easily adapt the design for mirrors of other shapes, or to use as a picture frame. This mirror originally had a plastic frame, which was removed with pliers.

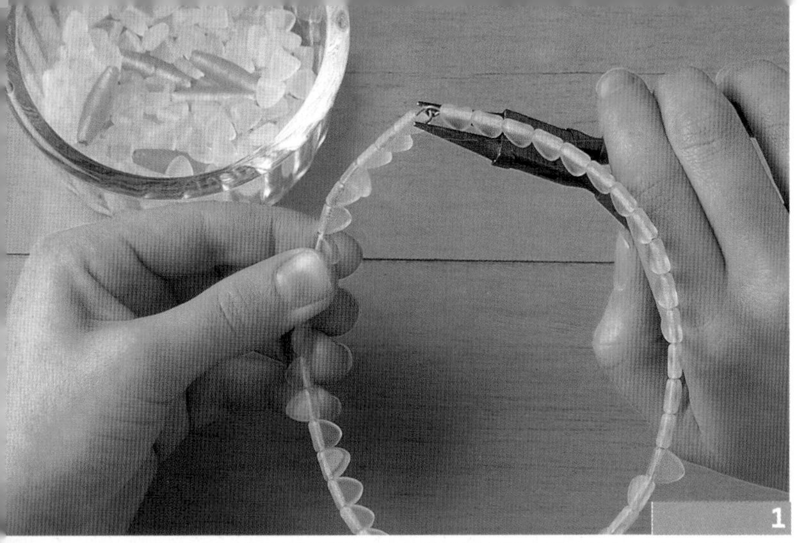

1

2

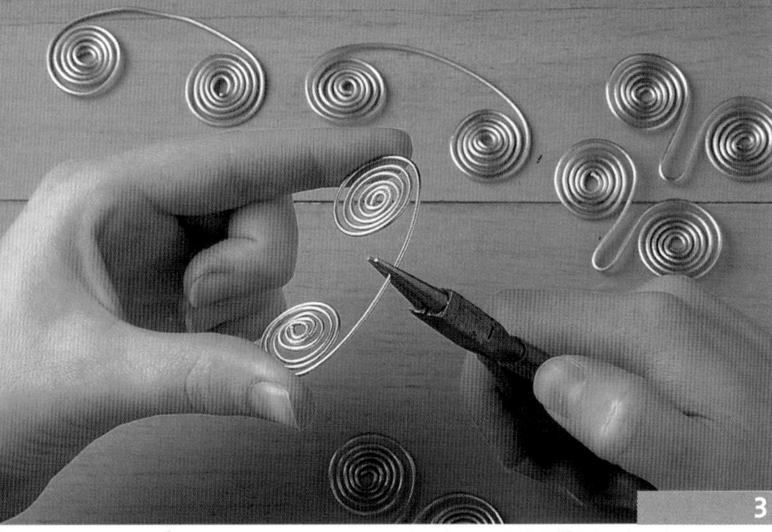

3

4

MATERIALS

Mirror without a frame
1mm galvanized wire
Frosted glass triangular edging beads
Frosted glass long beads
Fine binding wire
Enameled copper wire

TOOLS

Ruler
Wire cutters
Round-nose pliers

1

Measure the circumference of the mirror and cut a piece of wire a little longer than this. Thread triangular edging beads onto the wire, making sure the beads are not too tightly packed because you will need space between them for binding later. Use pliers to form a small loop at each end of the wire. Link them together and squeeze the loops closed.

2

Measure the radius of the circle you have just made, then add to it the length of two long beads. This is the required radius for the outer circle. Make the outer circle in the same way as the inner circle.

3

Form 12 double-ended spirals (see Basic Techniques, page 13). Grip the center of each wire firmly with pliers and push the spirals backward to achieve the shape shown.

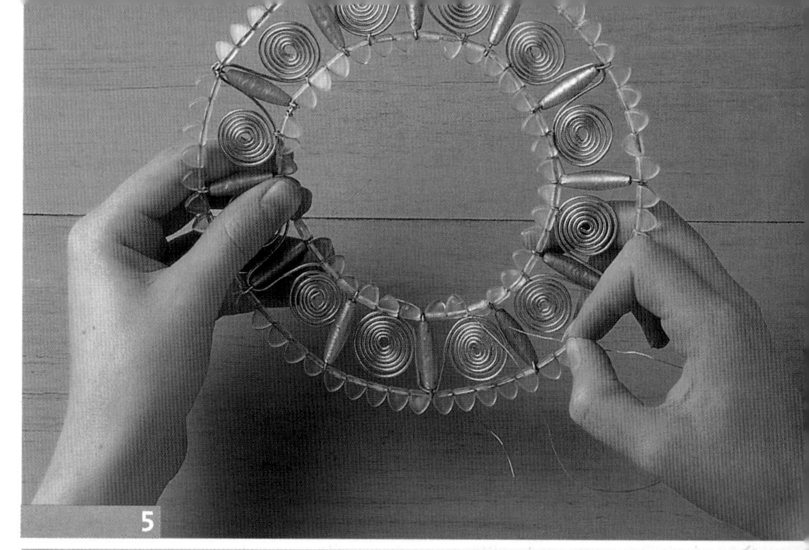

5

4

Thread a piece of wire through each long bead and use pliers to form a hook at each end. Position a long bead centrally between the spirals of each wire shape. Position a bead and a spiral between the inner and outer frames. Fix them in place by squeezing the outer hook closed around both the outer frame and the wire shape. Squeeze the bead's other hook around the inner frame. Position beads and spirals evenly all around the frame.

5

Use fine binding wire to secure the spirals to the inner frame, wrapping the wire around the base of the spiral and between pairs of triangular beads.

6

6

Place the mirror in position on the back of the frame. Make a triangular support from enameled copper wire, binding it around the base of the long beads at appropriate intervals. Form a loop for hanging, as shown.

CANDLESTICKS

These distinctive candlesticks are made from a stack of frosted glass droplets stuck to the base of a drinking glass and wrapped randomly with florist's wire. A small section of copper pipe acts as a candleholder. You could use sea-washed glass collected from a beach in a similar way. Make sure you use a strong adhesive and allow each section to dry before adding the next one.

MATERIALS

(for each candlestick)
Florist's wire
2 shot glasses, one slightly larger than the other
Small section of copper pipe
Round frosted glass droplets
Strong glue

TOOLS

Miricle pliers
Round-nose pliers

1

Wrap wire around the larger shot glass to create a conical coil. Do not worry about wrapping the wire around the glass neatly; the candlestick looks best with a more haphazard arrangement of coils. Remove the finished cone of wire from the glass.

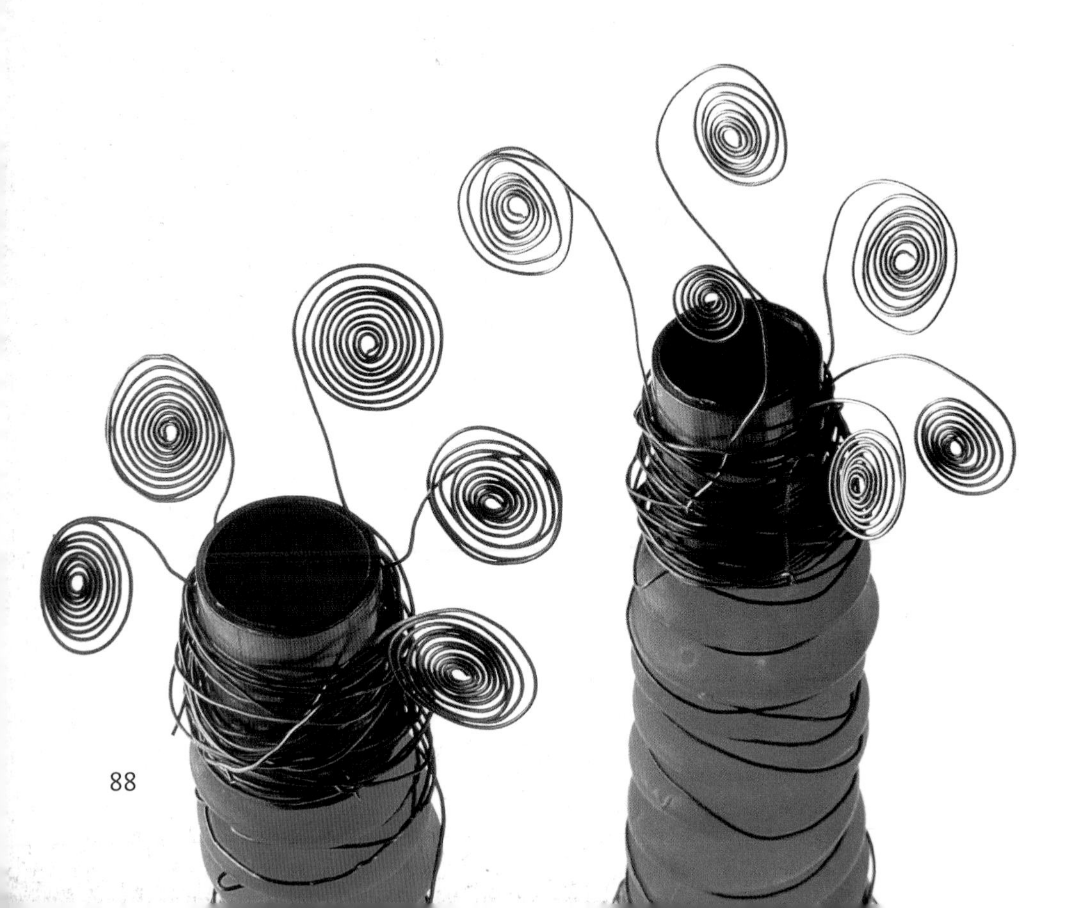

2

Coil wire around a short section of copper pipe. Make several wire spirals to decorate the top of the candlestick. Use miricle pliers to start the spiral but finish it by hand; florist's wire is soft enough to manipulate by hand and the slightly uneven spirals this produces are ideal.

3

Stick a glass droplet onto the bottom of the smaller shot glass using strong glue. Let it dry thoroughly, then glue another glass droplet on top of the first one. Again, let it dry before gluing another on top. Continue until you have reached the required height.

3

4

Glue the copper pipe on top of the tower of glass droplets and let it dry.

4

5

Place the large cone of wire over the candlestick. Spread out the top coils of wire so that they wind around the tiers of glass droplets at the top of the candlestick. Put the small coil of wire over the copper pipe, then bind the two coils of wire together.

5

6

Insert the ends of the wire spirals through the coils of wire around the copper pipe. Use round-nose pliers to bind the ends in place. Bend the spirals at attractive angles.

6

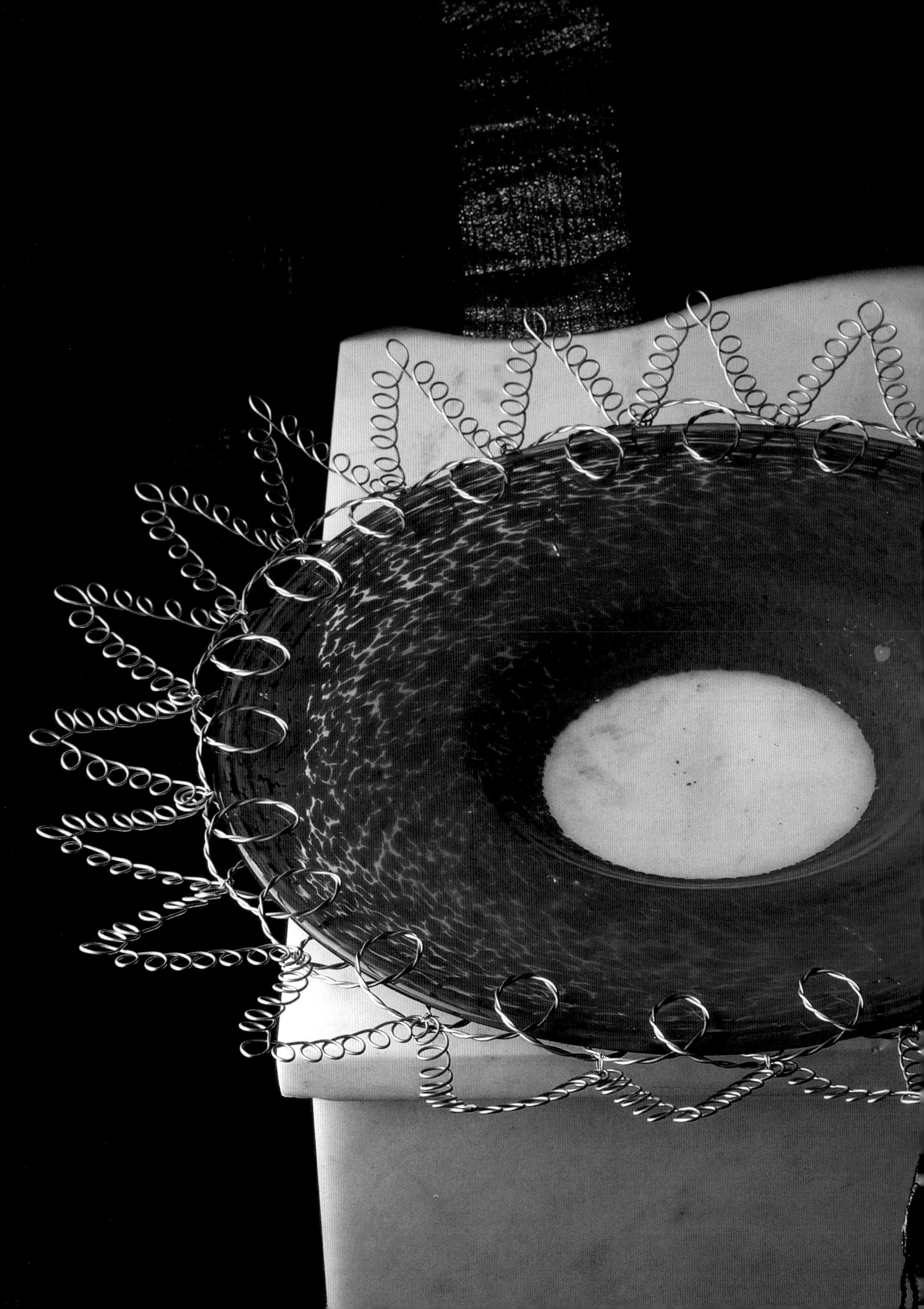

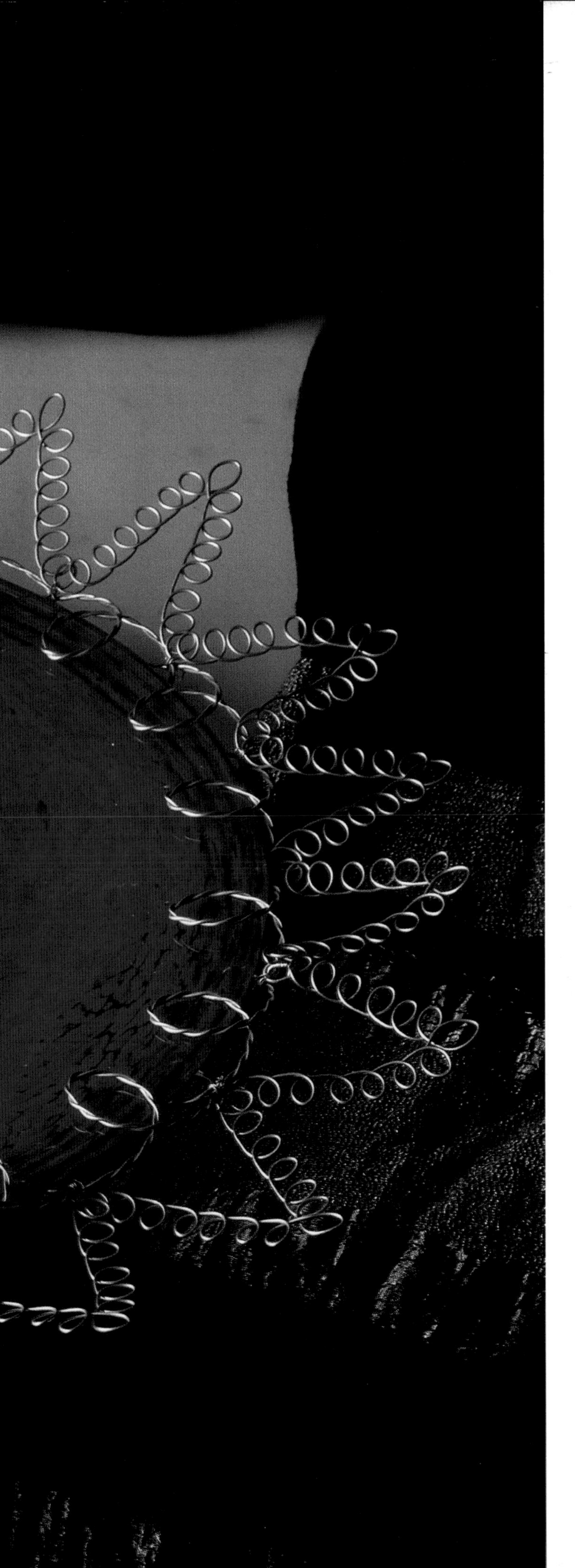

PLATE SURROUND

This surround can be used to add interest to a plain plate or to frame a special one for hanging on the wall. The surround is made from flattened coils of wire that grip the edge of the plate. Once you understand how the surround functions, you can try some variations, perhaps incorporating other decorative wire shapes or using enameled copper wire to add color.

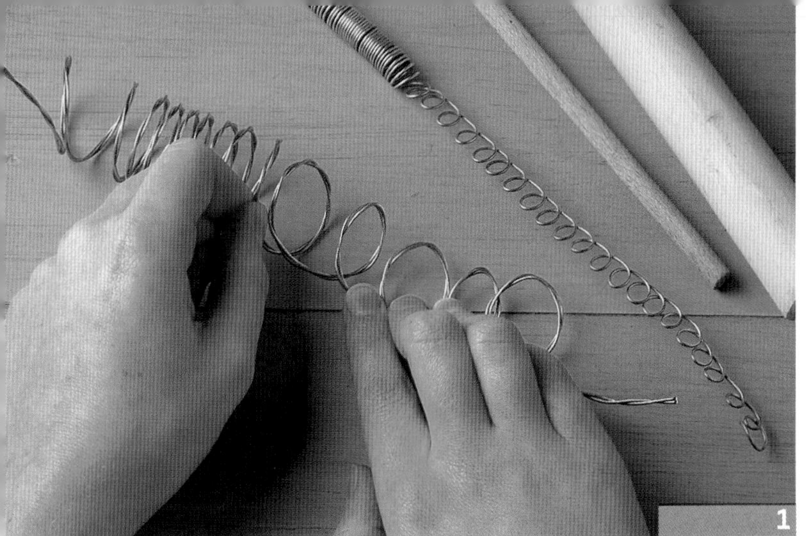

1

2

MATERIALS

0.9mm galvanized wire

Fine binding wire

TOOLS

Wire cutters

1/2in (1cm) and 1 1/2in (4cm) dowel

Chain-nose (snipe-nose) pliers

1

Make two flattened coils of wire (see Basic Techniques, page 14). Use the narrow dowel to make one of the coils from a single strand of wire, and the thicker dowel to make the other coil from two strands of wire twisted together. The length of the coils will depend on the size of the plate you wish to surround. Allow a length of expanded flattened coiled wire approx 2 1/2 times the circumference of your plate for the edging.

2

Bend the narrow flattened coil into a star-shaped edging that will fit around the circumference of the plate. Join the ends of the wire together by making small interlocking loops with pliers.

3

Insert the edge of the plate between the loops of the larger flattened coil, with the loops positioned alternately above and below the edge of the plate. When you have bent the coil into the correct size and shape, remove the plate and join the ends of the wire together by making small interlocking loops with pliers.

4

Position the star-shaped edging around the circular edging. Join the two elements together using fine binding wire at each point of contact. Tie the ends together securely and trim any excess wire.

5

If you want to hang the plate, make a hanging bracket by shaping a circle of wire to fit around the base of the plate. Use pliers to form a small loop at each end of the wire and link them together, squeezing the loops closed to secure. Cut five lengths of wire long enough to span between the base ring and the inner edge of the decorative surround. Use pliers to form a hook at both ends of each wire. Attach one end of four of the wires to the base ring, squeezing the hooks closed. Bend the remaining wire to form a U-shaped hanging hook.

6

Insert the plate into the decorative surround, then turn it over and position the base ring on the back. Connect the loose ends of the four wires on the base ring to the decorative frame, squeezing the hooks closed. Attach the hanging loop to the base ring, as shown.

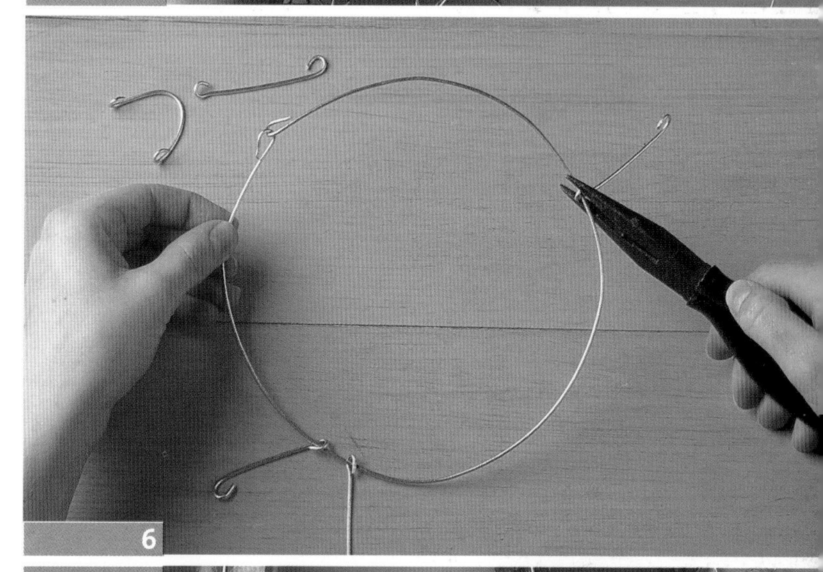

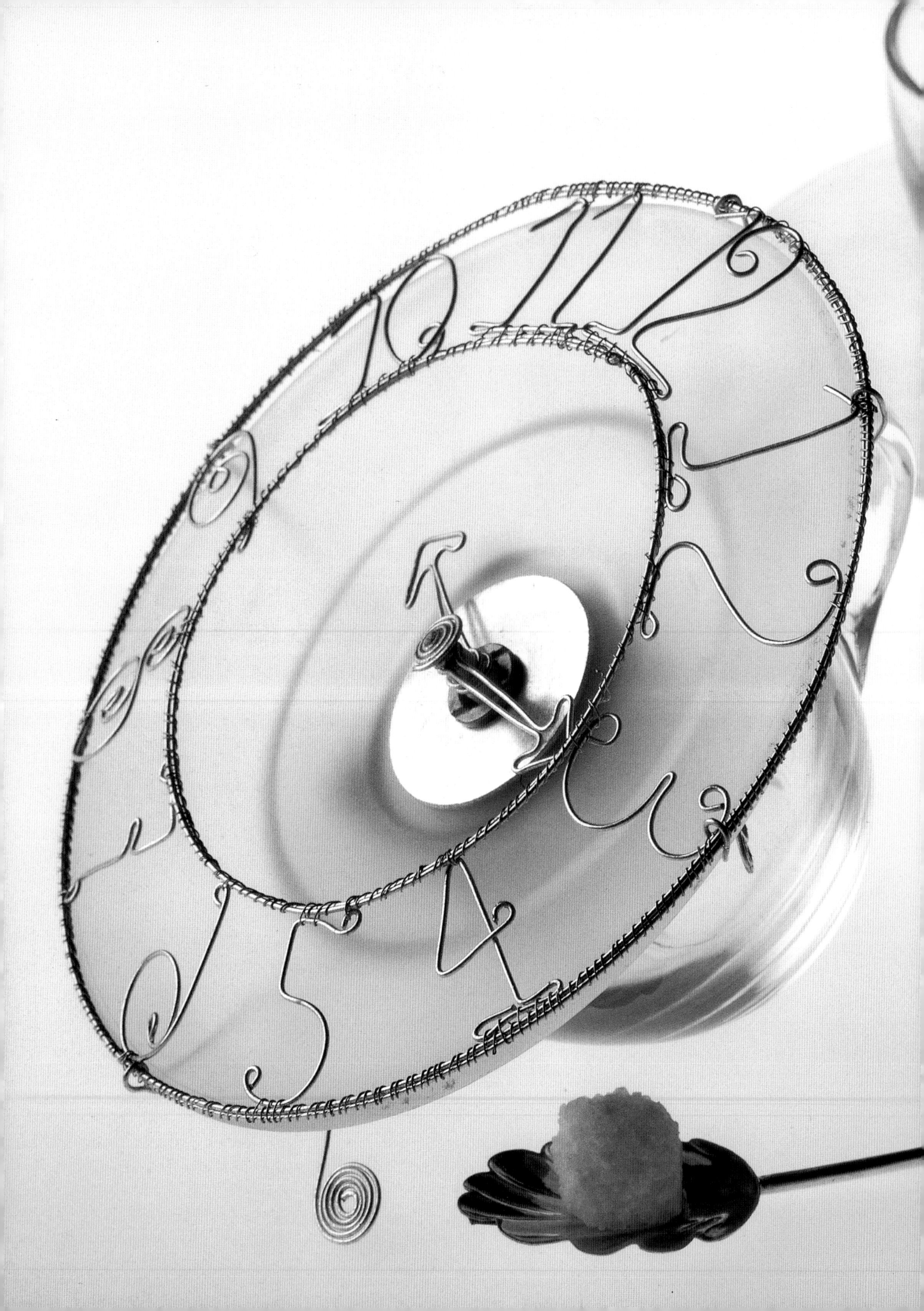

CONTEMPORARY CLOCK

This contemporary-looking clock is cunningly constructed using an ordinary glass teacup and saucer. Clock mechanisms can be purchased from craft stores or specialist suppliers, or you can dismantle a ready-made clock. Make sure the central shank is long enough to project through the saucer, taking the depth of the saucer into account. Glass drill bits are available from hardware stores.

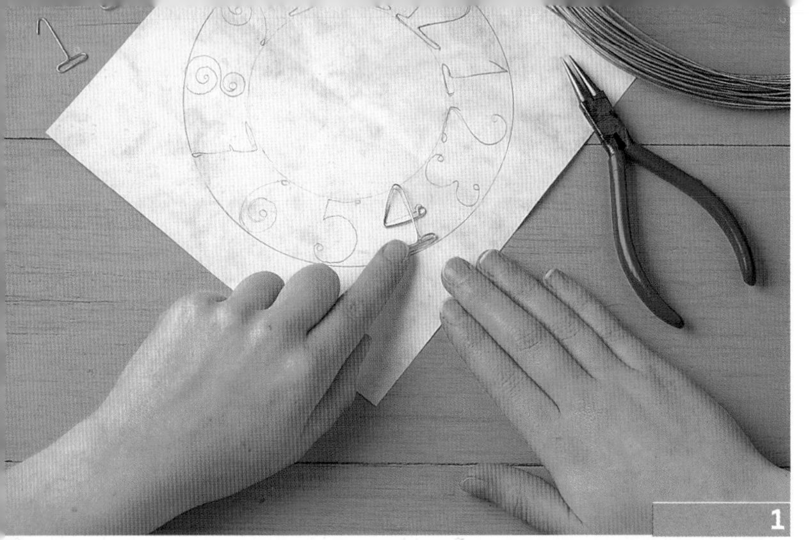

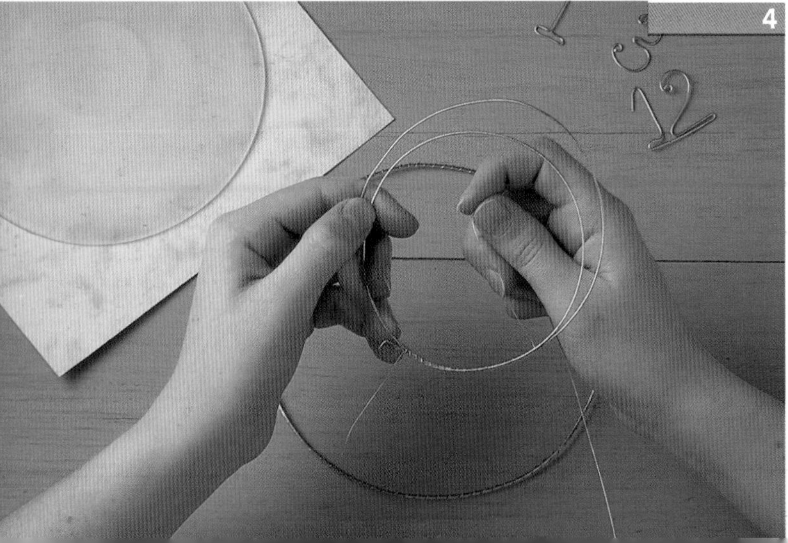

MATERIALS

Glass teacup and saucer
0.9mm galvanized wire
Clock mechanism
Fine binding wire

TOOLS

Pencil, paper, and compass
Wire cutters
Round-nose pliers
Chain-nose (snipe-nose) pliers
Glass drill bit and drill
Masking tape

1

Place the saucer face down on a piece of paper and draw around it. Find the center point of the circle and use a compass to draw an inner circle approximately 3in (7.5cm) smaller than the first one. Fold the paper into quarters through the center point. Sketch the numbers of the clock face between the two circles in such a way that each one is formed from one continuous line. Make sure the numbers are evenly positioned around the circle. Use round-nose and chain-nose (snipe-nose) pliers to shape the galvanized wire into numbers, using the numbers you have drawn as a template.

2

You may need to make several attempts before you achieve numbers you are happy with, but the end result will be worth it. Remember to make all parts of each number from a single piece of wire, including the numbers 10, 11, and 12.

3

Remove the hands from the clock mechanism, taking note of how they are assembled. Shape two arrows from galvanized wire to form new hands; remember to make the minute hand longer than the hour hand. Make sure that their bases fit into the respective hour and minute positions on the shank.

4

Form a circle of wire to fit the rim of the saucer with the ends overlapping by at least half the circumference. Join the ends with fine binding wire. Make another circle to fit the inner ring on the template, again with the ends overlapping.

5

Wrap fine binding wire around the smaller circle, incorporating the bases of the numbers in the correct positions. Wrap binding wire evenly all around the circle, in between the numbers as well along the numbers' bases. Bind the outer circle into position around the top of the numbers in the same way.

6

Make brackets to connect the wire clock face to the cup and saucer by cutting five lengths of wire long enough to reach from the rim of the saucer to the rim of the cup when the saucer is sitting on the cup. Use round-nose pliers to form a hook at one end of each wire and a spiral at the other end, as shown.

7

Attach the hooks of two of the wires to the outer circle of the clock face on either side of the number 12. Attach the hook from one of the remaining three wires to the numbers 3, 6, and 9. Squeeze the hooks closed around the rim to secure.

8

Cut some wire long enough to wrap twice around the rim of the cup. Use round-nose pliers to form a small spiral at each end. Thread the wire through the cup handle and around the cup. Twist the wire with a half turn to secure it tightly around the cup.

5

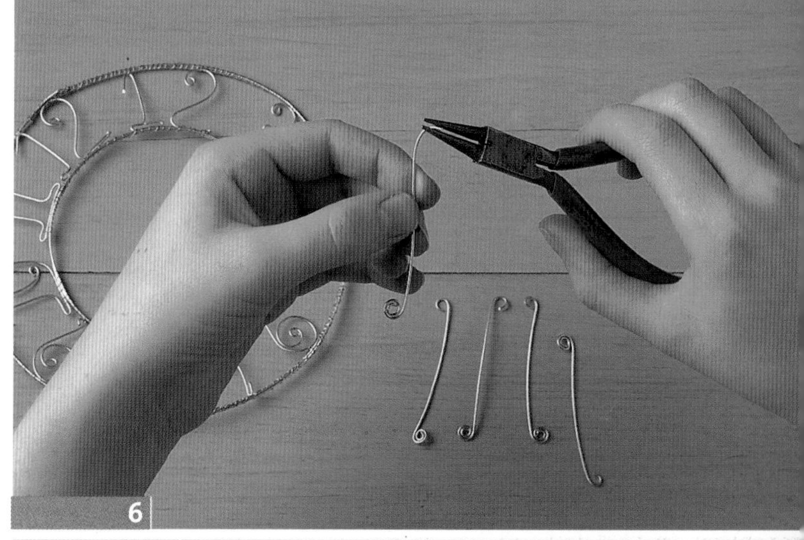
6

7

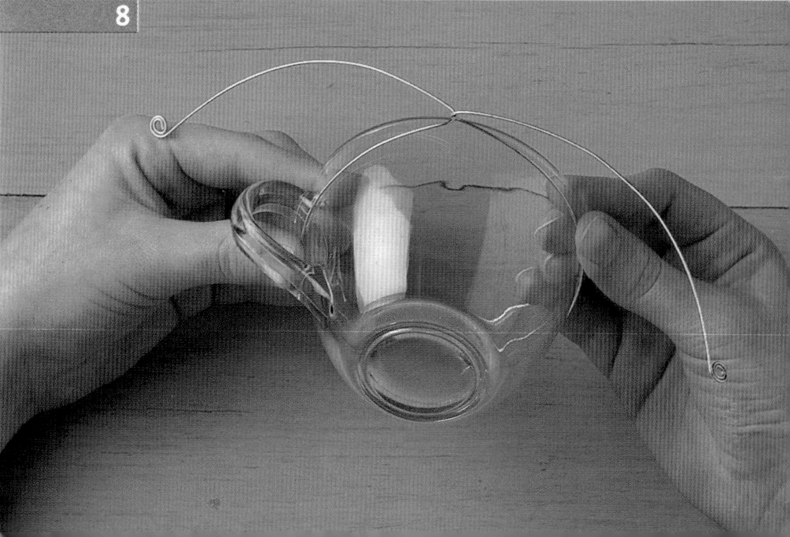
8

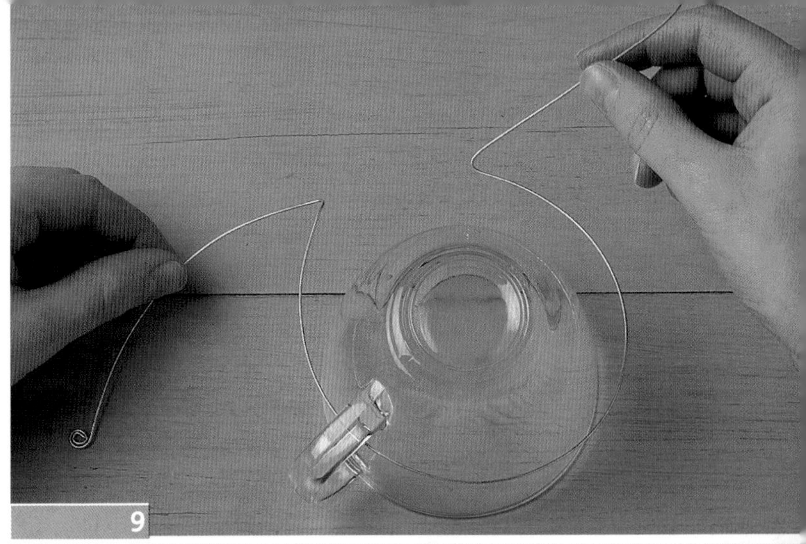

9

Unfurl the twist in the wire and remove it from the cup. This wire will act as a base for attaching the clock face and saucer to the cup later. Put the cup and the wire ring to one side.

10

Using a glass drill bit of the correct size for the clock shank, carefully drill a hole in the center of the saucer. Remember to place some masking tape over the area to be drilled and observe the safety precautions outlined (see Basic Techniques, page 17).

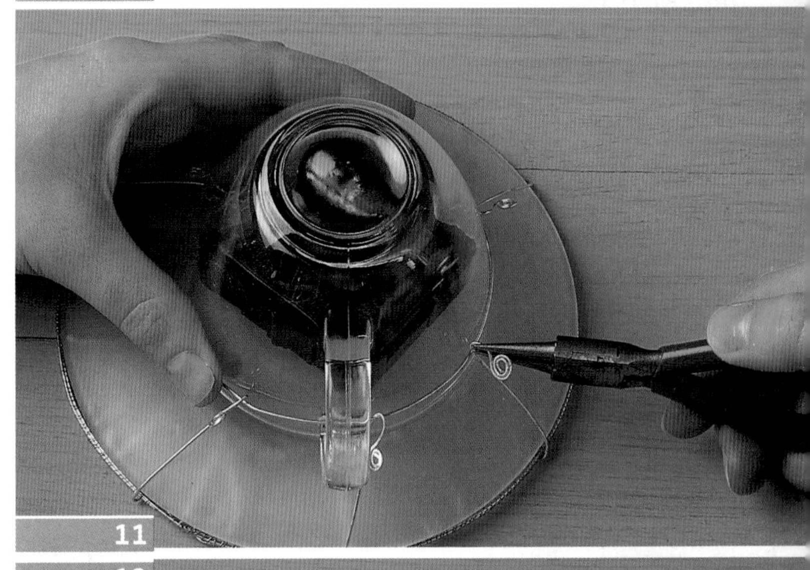

11

Insert the shank of the clock mechanism through the hole in the saucer from the back and attach it with the connecting screw. The mechanism should be held securely in place. Lay the saucer on top of the wire clock face, making sure they are both face down. Position the cup on top of the saucer with the handle at the 12 o'clock position. Put the wire ring around the cup once more but do not hook it in place. Pull back the wire brackets from the rim of the clock face and thread them through the wire ring around the cup, bending each one back as shown.

12

Hook the ends of the wire ring together around the cup at the 6 o'clock position. Wind the excess wire into equal-sized spirals to act as the feet for the clock to rest on.

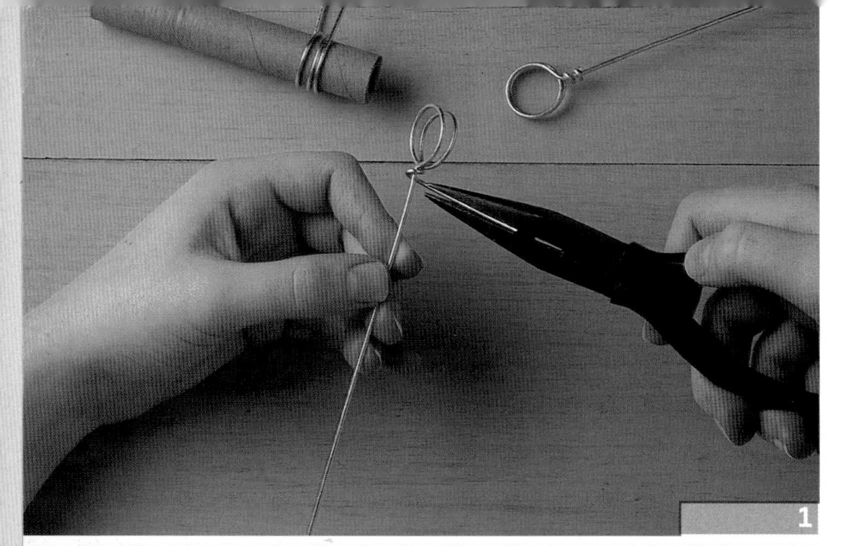

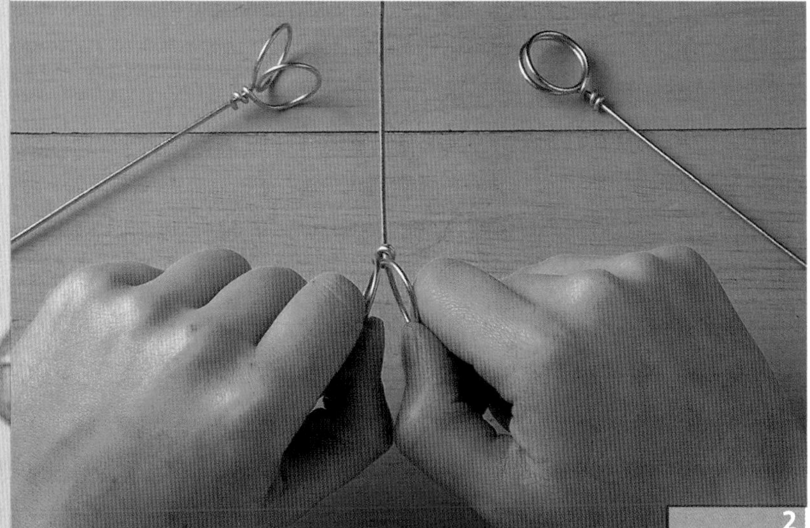

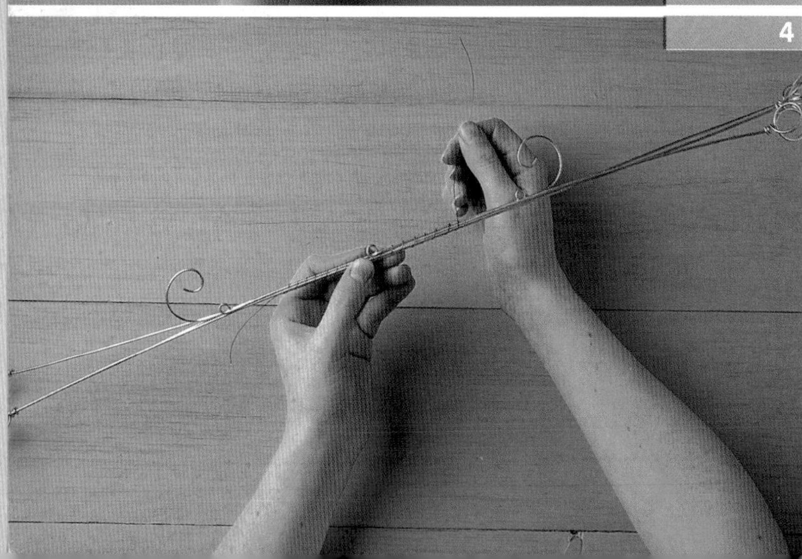

MATERIALS

0.8mm and 1.6mm galvanized wire
6 regular-sized marbles
Fine binding wire
3 large marbles
3 screws

TOOLS

Wire cutters
2 different thicknesses of dowel (to make holders for the large and regular marbles)
Chain-nose (snipe-nose) pliers
Round-nose pliers

1

Cut three 24in (60cm) lengths of the thickest galvanized wire. Make a holder for the regular sized marbles at both ends of each piece of wire by winding the end of the wire twice around a suitably sized piece of dowel or similar item. Finish by wrapping the end of the wire around the base of the marble holder using chain-nose (snipe-nose) pliers. Cut off any excess wire.

2

Spread the two rings of each marble holder apart and click a marble into place between them. Repeat this at each end of all three pieces of wire.

3

Cut an 18in (45cm) length of thick galvanized wire and use round-nose pliers to form three small loops evenly spaced along its length. These will be used to house the screws that will hold the rack to the wall. Bend the ends of the wire upward into a neat curve, as shown.

4

Join the four lengths of wire together loosely with fine binding wire. The binding wire will be removed later but helps to keep four wires in place while you are working with them. These four wires form the main horizontal rail of the hanging rack.

5

Make three holders for the large marbles from the thick galvanized wire. Make a split ring for each marble as described in steps 1 and 2, but do not bind around the base of them yet. Make a single wire hoop for each marble by wrapping a length of wire once around the dowel used in step 1.

6

Click the marble into place between the each split ring and then slip a wire hoop over the middle of the marble.

7

Tightly bind the four wire ends of each large marble holder together using the finer galvanized wire. These will form the shanks of the hooks.

8

Bind each shank until it is long enough to form a hook, then bend the remaining loose wires apart at an angle of 90 degrees. Trim these wires to about 1in (2.5cm). These will later be bound into the horizontal rail of the hanging rack.

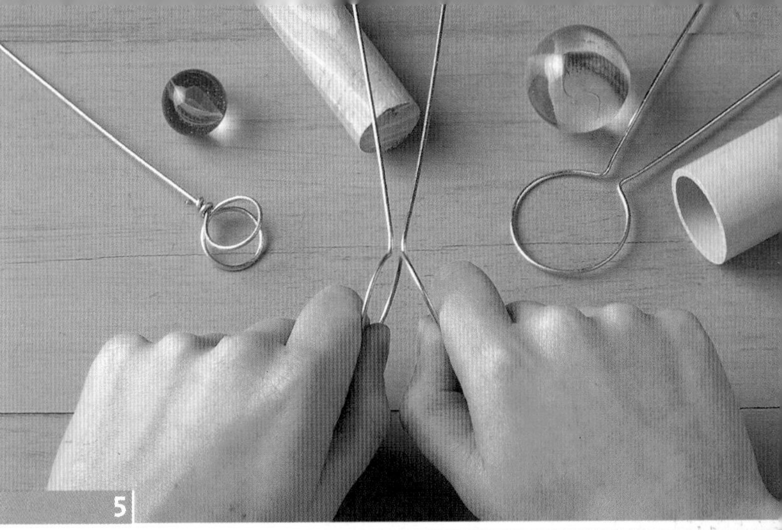
5

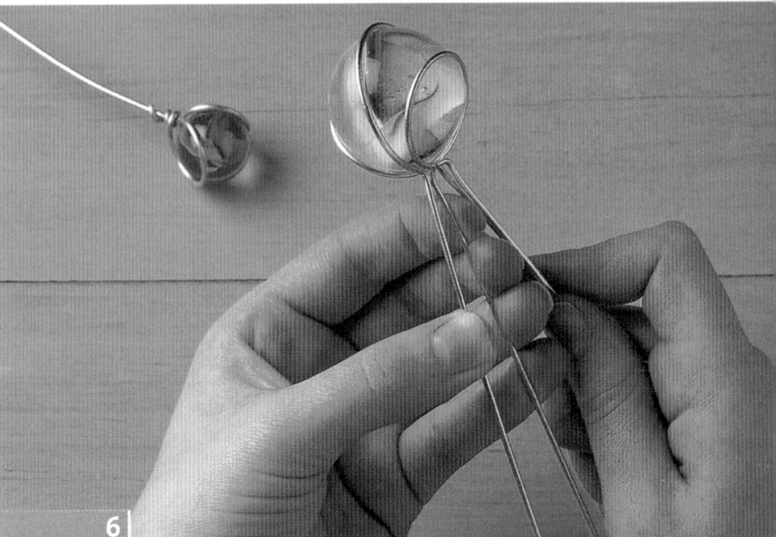
6

7

8
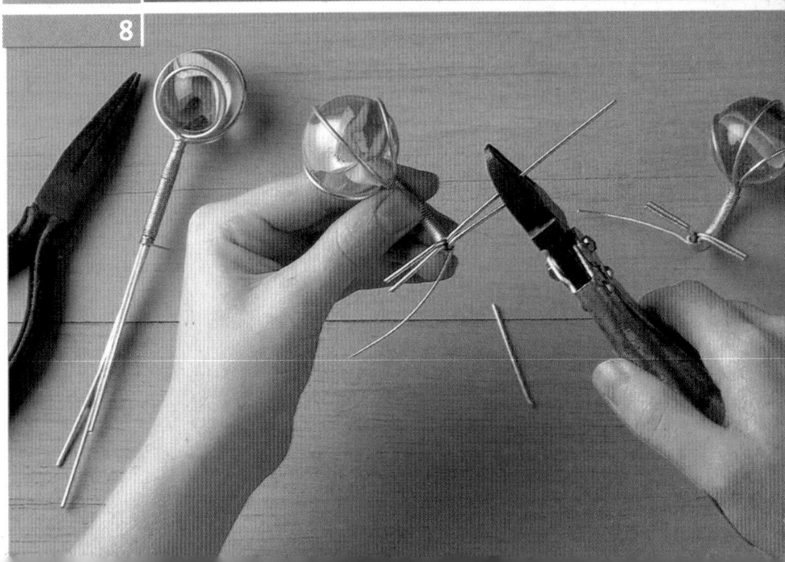

9

Form each hook into the curved shape by bending it around the thick dowel.

10

Bind the finished hooks to the horizontal rail using the narrow galvanized wire, positioning each hook directly below a screw loop.

11

Continue binding the hooks in place, removing the fine binding wire you used to hold the four wires of the horizontal rail together as you go.

12

Spread out the decorative end wires of the horizontal rail and screw the finished rack to a wall.

9

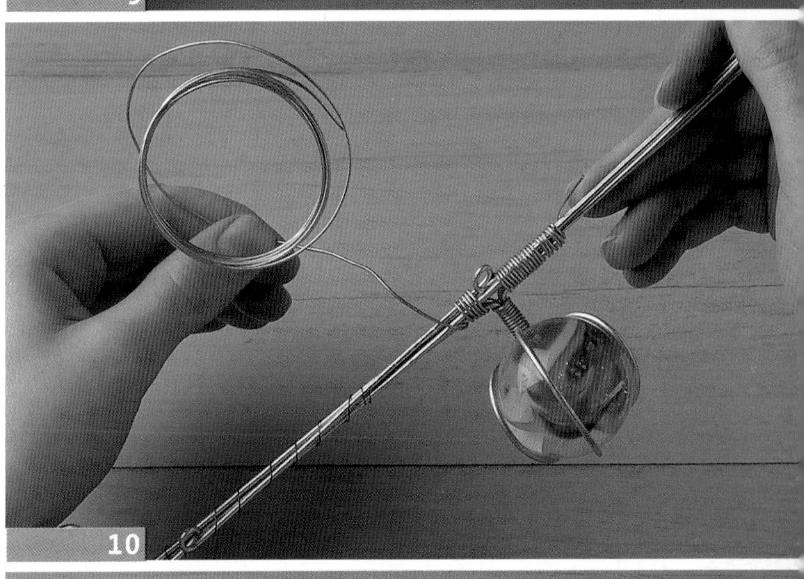

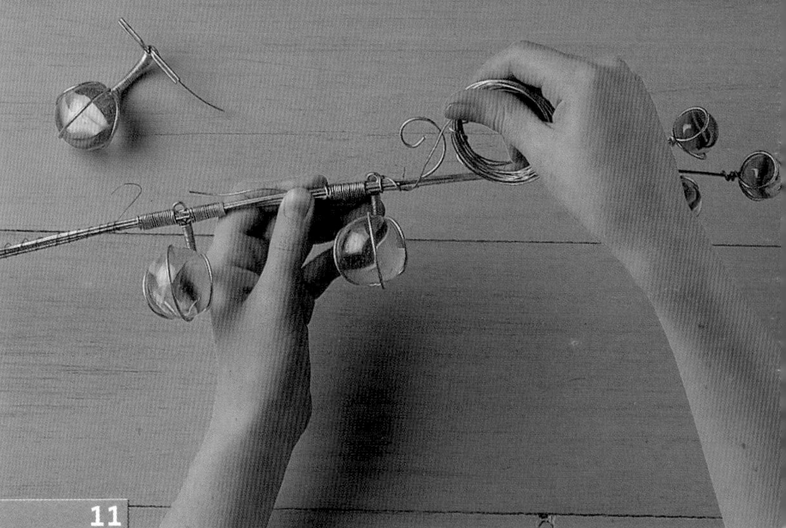

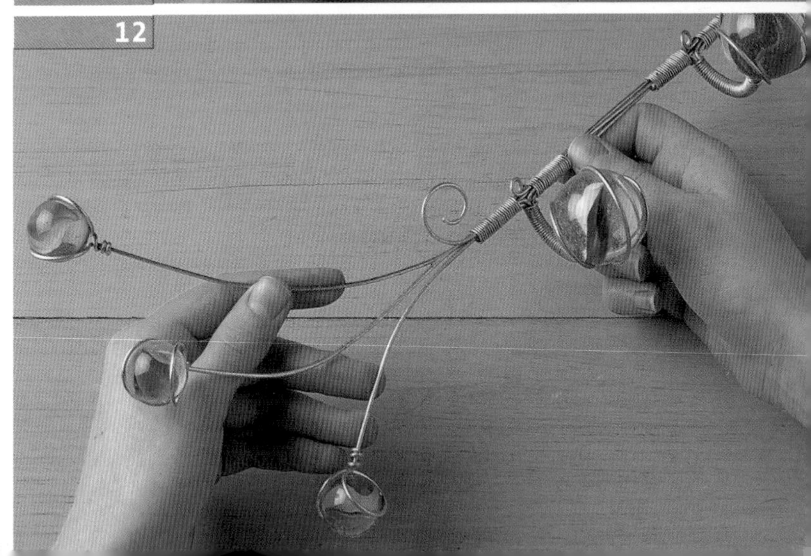

ARABESQUE LAMPSHADE

The lampshade is made from lots of individual elements, so this is a project for the more experienced wire worker. Each element is not difficult to make, but time and patience are needed when binding them together to construct the shape. Use beads to embellish the wire and add color. The lampshade looks best around a soft-colored bulb or placed over a small ready-made shade.

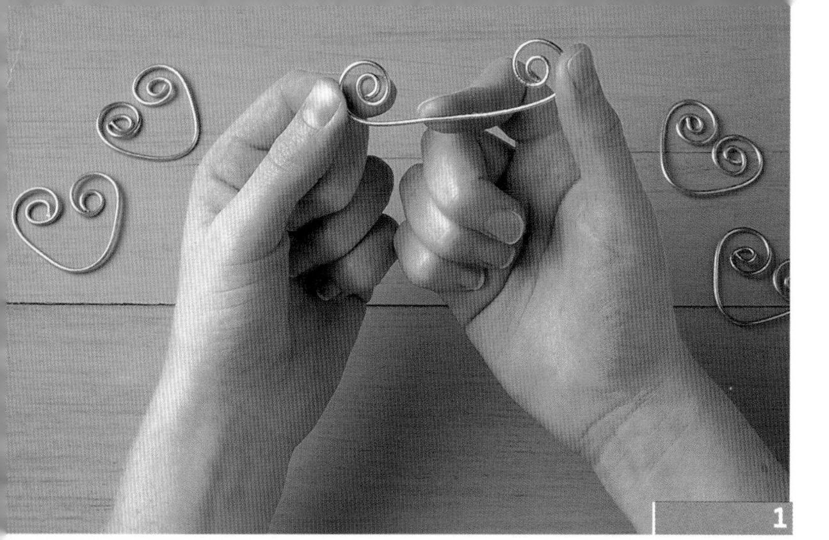

MATERIALS

1mm and 1.5mm galvanized wire
Fine binding wire
Assortment of beads
Lamp fitting
Jewelry jump rings

TOOLS

Wire cutters
Variety of pliers, including round-nose
Various thicknesses of dowel, including 2½in (6cm)
Gig (see page 15)

1

Cut eight 8in (20cm) lengths of 1.5mm wire. Use pliers to form each wire into a double-ended spiral, then bend them into heart shapes (see Basic Techniques, page 13).

2

Cut thirty 10in (25cm) lengths of 1.5mm wire and use pliers to form them into scrolls (see page 13). Make ten into short scrolls (see left-hand side of picture) and twenty into long scrolls (see right side).

3

Cut ten 13in (33cm) lengths of 1.5mm wire. Form each length into a double-ended spiral, as before. Push the ends of the spirals together to form a gentle dome shape (see left-hand side of picture). Cut eleven 11in (28cm) lengths of 1.5mm wire and form each one into an open spiral approximately 1½in (4cm) in diameter (see Basic Techniques, page 16). Bend the last bit of wire into a loop in the opposite direction (see right-hand side of picture).

4

Use fine binding wire to suspend beads inside each heart shape. Insert beads onto the center wire of the open spirals and short scrolls. You may have to cut off a little wire at the center to do this.

5

Cut 20in (50cm), 24in (60cm), and 27in (68cm) lengths of 1.5mm wire. Thread approximately 30 large beads onto the longest piece, 20 large beads onto the medium piece, and 25 small beads onto the shortest piece. Bend all three wires into circles, using pliers to form interlocking loops at the ends. Squeeze the loops closed.

6

Make a flattened coil 24in (60cm) long and 1in (2 1/2cm) wide using 1.5mm wire (see Basic Techniques, page 14). Use 1.5mm wire to make a length of wiggly wire, 23in (58cm) long and in 3/4in (2cm) wide (see page 15).

7

Coil some 1.5mm wire around 2 1/2in (6cm) dowel or something similar. Remove the coil from the dowel and extend the loops out flat, as shown, until you have a 10-petaled flower shape. Use pliers to form a small loop at each end of the wire, link them together, and squeeze the loops closed. This will form the top of the lampshade.

8

Cut a piece of 1.5mm wire long enough to wrap around the lamp fitting two or three times. Wrap the wire around the fitting and use pliers to bend the ends of the wire out on opposite sides at a 45-degree angle. You may find this easiest with parallel pliers. Cut off the excess wire, leaving about 1/2in (1cm) on each side. Use pliers to form the ends into loops.

9

Position the wire lamp fitting in the center of the petaled

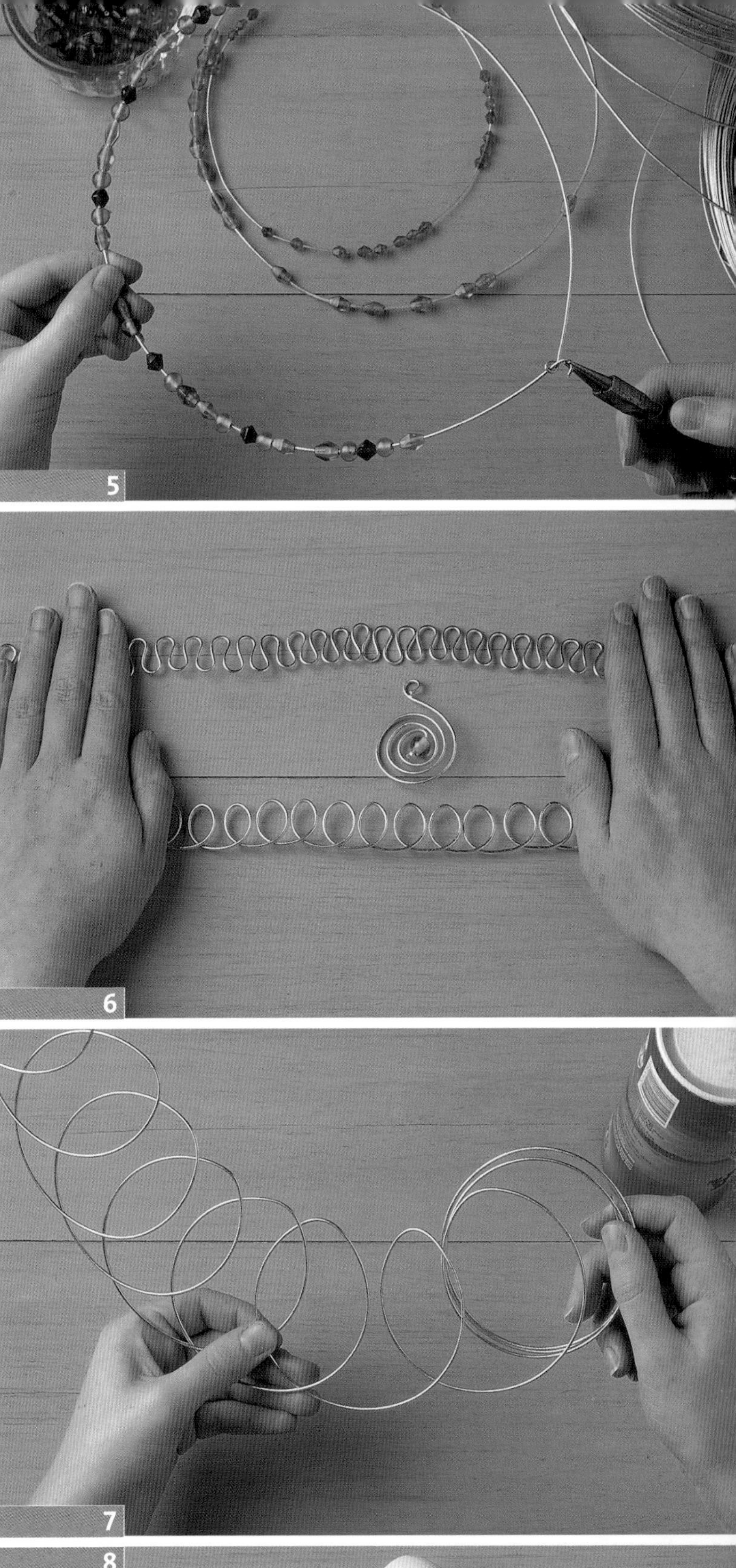

9

top section, connecting the links of the wire fitting to the petals and squeezing them closed to secure.

10

10

Place the largest beaded hoop around the petaled top section. Position the domed spirals at the tip of each petal, binding them onto the hoop and petaled top section with short lengths of 1mm wire. Make sure you arrange the beads evenly between the shapes around the hoop.

11

11

Place a short scroll between pairs of long scrolls, binding them together with 1mm wire at their contact points.

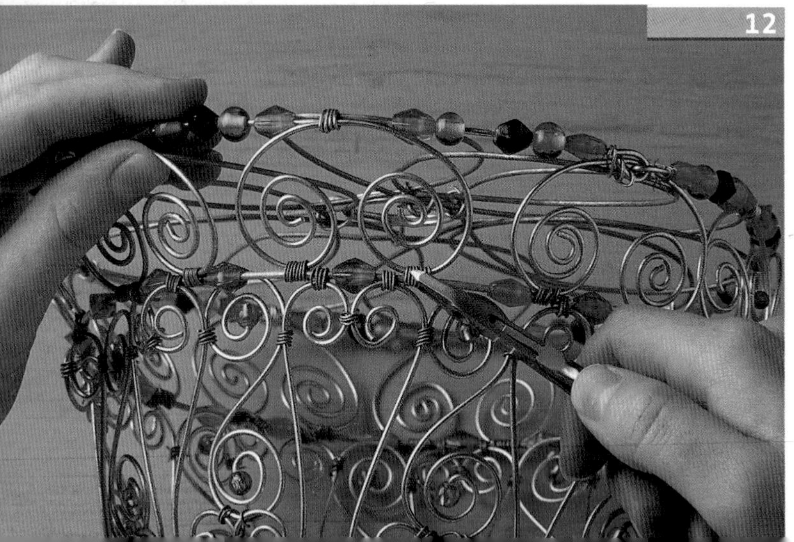
12

12

Bind the medium-size hoop to the base of the domed spirals using 1mm wire. Space the beads evenly, as shown. Next, bind the three-part scrolls you formed in step 11 to the medium-sized hoop using 1mm wire.

13

Using fine binding wire, attach the smallest hoop to

the base of the scrolls, making sure that the beads are evenly spaced.

14

Bind the flattened coil to the small hoop, then attach the open spirals to the base of the coil with fine binding wire. Attach the length of wiggly wire beneath these spirals, as shown.

15

Cut eight 2in (5cm) lengths of 1mm wire. Use pliers to form a hook at one end, suspend a droplet bead from this, and squeeze the hook closed. Thread a bead onto the remaining wire and form a loop at the top, cutting off any excess wire. Link a beaded wire to the base of each heart, then squeeze the loop closed.

16

Attach the beaded hearts to the bottom of the wiggly wire using jump rings, as shown. Make sure you squeeze the jump rings firmly closed. You can dangle more beads from the wire lampshade for additional decoration if you wish; look at the picture on page 106 for inspiration.

INDEX

RESOURCES AND ACKNOWLEDGMENTS

Wire, pliers and other materials used in this book are readily available at most local hardware, home improvement and craft retailers. Below is home office information for finding the store closest to you or check your phone directory for local suppliers. Also listed are some specialty suppliers that you can contact for mail order service.

Beadworks
North American General Offices
In the US: (800) 232-3761
www.beadworks.com

The Building Box
In Canada: (877) 277-3651
www.thebuildingbox.com

Home Depot (US and Can)
In the US: (770) 433-8211
In Canada: (800) 668-226
www.homedepot.com

Lowe's Home
Improvement Warehouse
In the US: (800) 44-LOWES
www.lowes.com

MacPherson Craft Supplies
In Canada: (519) 284-1741
www.macphersoncrafts.com

Menards
In the US: (612) 946-5380

Michaels Stores, Inc.
In the US: (800) MICHAELS
www.michaels.com

Paramount Wire Co.
In the US: (973) 672-0500
www.parawire.com

Paul Gesswein & Co Inc
In the US: (800) 243-4466
In Canada: (800) 263-6106
www.gesswein.com

Revy Home & Garden Warehouses and Home Centers
In western Canada: (604) 882-6200
In eastern Canada: (416) 241-8844
www.revy.com

Wire Mart International
In the US: (800) 829-8936
www.wiremart.com

Thank you to Andrew Gillimore for his inspired projects and general help: name plaque, glass carrier, tea glasses and hanging rack.
Thanks to 'The Holding Company' (0207 352 7495) for the silver mesh bags shown on page 42.